FOREWORD

Flint blades dating to the Palaeolithic period, together with stone tools left by Mesolithic communities that inhabited the upland areas encompassing the modern town some 11,500 years ago, represent the earliest physical remains of Rochdale's illustrious history. The town was probably established during the Anglo-Saxon period, and was sufficiently important by 1251 to be granted a Royal Charter. It flourished through the post-medieval period as a centre of Lancashire's woollen trade, being noted in the early 18th century for its many wealthy wool merchants. Rochdale rose to prominence as a leading mill town in the 19th century, becoming one of the first industrial townscapes in the world and widely acknowledged as the birthplace of the Co-operative movement.

An incredible range of archaeological research carried out over many decades helps to illustrate the captivating story of Rochdale's evolution from prehistoric times to the 21st century. Salford Archaeology is to be congratulated for synthesising this huge body of archaeological evidence to provide a context within which to appreciate the remains of the 19th-century townscape that were excavated in 2019–20 as part of the Riverside development. This regeneration scheme has made a significant contribution to an ambitious plan to rejuvenate the town centre that was implemented by the Rochdale Development Agency in the late 2000s. Delivery was focussed initially on creating a new public transport interchange and was followed in 2015–16 by a major project that uncovered a section of the River Roch and the historic stone bridge that had been hidden from view for much of the 20th century. More recently, the Rochdale Development Agency secured significant funding from the National Lottery Heritage Fund to restore the magnificent town hall and the adjacent Broadfield Park Slopes together with the creation of new public realm in Town Hall Square, whilst the historic thoroughfare of Drake Street became the focus of a Heritage Action Zone programme. This wide-ranging regeneration has revitalised Rochdale town centre and has raised awareness of the town's fascinating heritage, which is reflected in the archaeological discoveries presented in this lavishly illustrated booklet.

IAN MILLER
COUNTY ARCHAEOLOGIST
GREATER MANCHESTER ARCHAEOLOGICAL ADVISORY SERVICE

GMAAS
Greater Manchester Archaeological Advisory Service

INTRODUCTION

On a cold winter's morning in January 2018, a 16-tonne machine under the direction of Graham Mottershead – a highly experienced archaeologist working for Salford Archaeology, a commercial archaeological practice based at the University of Salford – began digging into the surface of a desolate car park in the centre of Rochdale. The trench that Graham was opening was intended to establish what remained of buildings constructed when Rochdale was a thriving industrial town. The trench was not only the beginning of one of the most extensive archaeological investigations in Rochdale to date, but also part of an exciting scheme to regenerate Rochdale's town centre.

The excavations were undertaken ahead of a major redevelopment: Rochdale Riverside. This project intended to contribute towards the renewal of Rochdale's town centre by delivering a new retail, leisure and commercial complex. The construction of these new buildings would require deep foundation trenches which would potentially damage or remove any archaeological remains that were present beneath the ground. Before the redevelopment, the site contained a range of mostly dilapidated mid-20th-century buildings including a bus station, a multi-storey car park, council offices, healthcare facilities and a car dealership. The harsh urban environment was dominated by a busy and noisy road gyratory system, with pedestrians channelled along awkward aerial walkways.

Above: An archaeologist from Salford Archaeology prepares an evaluation trench at Rochdale Riverside Phase 2 in June 2020

Below: Clay tobacco pipe stem inscribed 'FOOT BALL PIPE', c. 1900, from Rochdale Riverside site (© University of Salford)

Opposite: The remains of the Congregational Church on the corner of Milton Street and Smith Street, exposed in February 2018, looking south-west (© University of Salford)

0   10 cm

A delivery plan to rejuvenate the town centre was set in motion by the Rochdale Development Agency in the early 21st century. The first step of this regeneration began with the construction of a new public transport interchange, completed in 2013. Some key objectives of the renewal programme were to improve Rochdale's natural environment, and to increase the quality of the borough's heritage assets. Therefore, in 2015 and 2016, parts of the coverings that had sealed the River Roch for almost one hundred years were removed, giving the river's ecosystems a chance to recover and revealing historic bridges that had been lost to view.

As part of the planning process, the Greater Manchester Archaeological Advisory Service (GMAAS) requires due consideration to be afforded to potential archaeological remains that could be damaged or removed during redevelopment work. This typically involves a desk-based study in the first instance to establish the potential for archaeological remains to survive, often followed by intrusive investigation via evaluation trenching and a final stage of excavation, all funded by the developer. Many of the archaeological discoveries presented in this booklet derived from developer-funded projects, although the work of local societies and community-led excavations have also made important contributions to the archaeological history of Rochdale.

While it is by no means intended to be a comprehensive account, this booklet presents aspects of Rochdale's history through the lens of the archaeological investigations that have been carried out in the borough over the last 100 years or so. This booklet illustrates the value of conducting archaeological research, since it frequently reveals details about a place's past that historical documentary sources do not record.

The understanding of Rochdale's prehistoric past is derived entirely from archaeological investigation. Much of our knowledge of Rochdale's first inhabitants comes from artefacts collected by the area's first archaeologists (although they would have called themselves antiquarians or geologists), who found flint tools on the nearby upland moors during the second half of the 19th century. In recent years, fieldwork undertaken by the Littleborough Archaeological Society and Newcastle University has continued this research, confirming Mesolithic occupation in the area. Artefacts associated with the later prehistoric period have also been discovered in the borough of Rochdale.

Our knowledge of Roman occupation in Rochdale is patchy as it is based solely on artefacts discovered by chance, often during building work carried out in the 19th century. No structural remains – apart from the hotly debated possible Roman road over Blackstone Edge – have been found that might point to a Roman settlement in Rochdale. However, it can't be ruled out that traces of Roman occupation have been obscured or destroyed by building work during the industrial era.

No archaeological evidence has been found pertaining to the period between the end of the Roman occupation and the Norman invasion either, apart from a tentatively dated wall in the graveyard of St Chad's Church. Again, this situation probably reflects destruction by industrial-period development and a lack of archaeological investigation rather than a genuine absence of pre-Norman inhabitation.

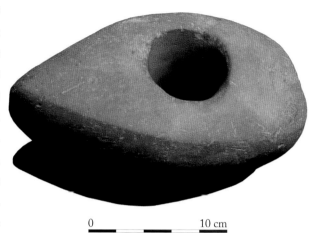

0   10 cm

Above: A Bronze Age axe hammer from Lowhouse Fold, Milnrow

Below: The nave of St Chad's Church, c. 1970 (courtesy of Touchstones Rochdale)

Opposite: An example of a Georgian building at 17 Yorkshire Street photographed c. 1900. Until recently this building was used as a Lloyds Bank (courtesy of Touchstones Rochdale)

The Domesday Book records land holdings both before and after William's conquest of the region in 1070, proving that the area was occupied by then. This booklet explains the archaeological evidence from this period discovered at St Chad's Church and Rochdale Castle. The latter was surveyed in the early 19th century and subjected to archaeological excavation using modern techniques in the 1980s and early 21st century. However, knowledge of medieval Rochdale is still largely conjectural and few of the investigations located in the centre of the modern town have revealed any medieval remains or artefacts.

Surprisingly, as will be explained, despite a significant amount of archaeological work undertaken in Rochdale, very little evidence associated with the post-medieval period has been uncovered. This is again probably because of later 18th- and 19th-century development, which had disturbed or obscured earlier remains. In several instances, post-medieval occupation is represented by horticultural activity, for example at Rochdale Town Hall and Rochdale Riverside. In both of these examples, industrial-era buildings had been constructed on the extensive grounds of large post-medieval halls. Fortunately, because Rochdale has some surviving late post-medieval buildings and because documentary material is abundant, there is a good understanding of the flavour of the town in this period.

Rochdale contained many buildings and structures characteristic of an industrialised town by the last decade of the 18th century. Archaeological investigations such as those undertaken by Oxford Archaeology North at River Street and Salford Archaeology's excavations at Kitchen Street have revealed the remains of Rochdale's industrial past, providing remarkable glimpses of an early 19th-century textile-engineering works and a tannery.

Left: Houses on the east side of Acker Street, photographed in 1970 (courtesy of Touchstones Rochdale)

Opposite: Volunteers and professional archaeologists from Salford Archaeology excavating and recording remains at Rochdale Town Hall Square, summer 2021, looking north towards St Chad's Church

Other aspects of industrial life have also been registered in Rochdale's archaeological record, such as the living conditions of working-class residents. Excavations conducted by Salford Archaeology at the Rochdale Riverside development provided fascinating insights into the intimate details of workers' houses. Compared to the low-quality, overcrowded housing that was built contemporaneously in similar inner-city parts of Manchester and Salford, it appears that in central Rochdale, at least in the examples excavated, the housing stock was of relatively high quality.

This booklet also draws on the numerous building surveys that have been conducted across Rochdale, often ahead of demolition. Possibly the most notable of these surveys was that undertaken by Oxford Archaeology North on the coverings spanning the River Roch in the town centre. The economic, cultural and religious practices of Rochdale's inhabitants are reflected in its buildings, and this booklet discusses investigations of several Nonconformist chapels and commercial structures.

Rochdale's economy began to contract after the First World War, and many buildings stood derelict by the mid-20th century. Attempts were made to rejuvenate the town with the clearance of low-quality housing and redevelopments in the town centre, whilst residential estates were built on the town's periphery to replace cleared housing and accommodate the rising population. Unfortunately, very little archaeological work was undertaken and it is conceivable that important archaeological sites were destroyed because consideration of archaeological remains had not yet been included in the planning process. Fortunately, as this booklet demonstrates, the current process enshrined in the National Planning Policy Framework has led to many archaeological investigations that have produced fascinating findings, shedding light on Rochdale's richly textured heritage.

As the climate warmed, the post-glacial landscape of north-west England, which had initially been covered by open birch scrub, began to be colonised by closed, mixed deciduous woodland, particularly on higher, drier land. The discovery of distinctive flint tools and features suggesting temporary occupation on the uplands to the north and east of Rochdale indicates that hunter-gatherers had inhabited the landscape around 11,500 years ago. It is likely that communities followed and hunted herds of deer as they migrated from lowland areas to upland pastures in the summer. The flint used to make tools by these nomadic groups appears to derive from the East Yorkshire region. While this could indicate the extent of the territory inhabited by these groups, this material may have ended up in the South Pennines as a result of exchange.

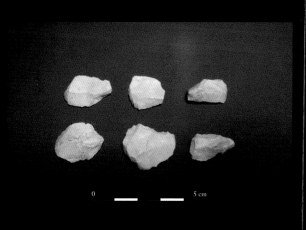

0 _____ _____ 5 cm

Top: Late upper Palaeolithic flint blades, from near Rochdale (courtesy of Touchstones Rochdale)

Bottom: Early Mesolithic flint scrapers found at Windy Hill, near Milnrow (courtesy of Touchstones Rochdale)

The means by which early prehistoric artefacts have been discovered around Rochdale has a fascinating history in itself, with worked flints first identified and collected by local amateur geologists in the 1870s. It seems that 'flinting' rapidly became a popular Sunday afternoon activity. In all weathers, enthusiasts searched for stone tools on the moors, which, due to pollution, were vegetated less extensively than today, making worked flints easier to spot. Individuals of particular note include Dr Henry Colley March who, between 1879 and 1895, was first able to confirm that layers of peat covered the Mesolithic flints, giving a clue to their great antiquity.

In the 1920s and 1930s, Francis Buckley – who had first encountered prehistoric flint tools whilst excavating trenches on the Western Front during the First World War – identified that the assemblages of flint tools he found could be categorised into two idiosyncratic morphologies which he attributed to different Mesolithic communities. More recent investigations at sites where flints were found in the 19th century, and others, continue to produce flint tools and evidence of hearths, improving an understanding of the activities undertaken by Mesolithic communities in upland areas near Rochdale.

Analysis of pollen from sediment core samples collected in the southern Pennines suggests that around 6,000 years ago, hunter-gatherers were modifying the environment, creating open woodland clearings by deliberately burning woodland. Woodland clearings were favourable to grazing herbivorous animals such as deer and aurochs (wild cattle). The clearings supported higher biomass of plant species favoured by herbivorous species, increasing their overall productivity. Additionally, once encouraged into the artificially engineered open spaces, game herds could be readily hunted. Clearance by burning would also have increased the range of plant species available for gathering by people.

Top: Bronze Age jet beads from Piethorne Brook (courtesy of Touchstones Rochdale)

Bottom: Neolithic polished stone axe from Newhey (courtesy of Touchstones Rochdale)

Communities practising rudimentary agriculture, involving the domestication of animals and the cultivation of cereals, moved into the area around 5,200 years ago. They brought with them new cultural activities such as making polished stone axes, like examples found at Castle Hill, Newhey and Wardle. However, arable cultivation does not appear to have been particularly intensive in the Rochdale area until around 4,300 years ago, when pollen evidence recovered from Rishworth Moor suggests that intensive woodland clearance and the cultivation of cereals took place.

The transitional era between the Neolithic (*c.* 4,000 to *c.* 2,500 BCE) and the Bronze Age (*c.* 2,500 to *c.* 800 BCE) is signalled by novel finds assemblages that include distinctive drinking beakers and metallurgy. It is believed that the usage of beaker vessels and metalworking are examples of cultural and economic practices that spread from continental Europe. A funeral cairn from this period at Wind Hill, north of Heywood, was found to contain a flint knife, a pebble hammer and a jet button.

Burial mounds such as that at Hades Hill in Wardle likely indicate the presence of settled farming communities in the region during the Bronze Age, and a number of casual finds of metalwork support this. Hades Hill was excavated in 1898, leading to the discovery of a collared urn containing cremated human bone and burnt flint implements, and flint arrowheads. A Bronze Age occupation site was excavated by Littleborough Archaeological Society at Piethorne Brook where worked flints, pottery, a shale ring and two jet beads were found. Although there was possible evidence for leatherworking, no structures were identified at the site.

New types of cultural artefacts, such as a bronze torc found at Mowroad in Calderbrook, pertain to the Iron Age, beginning in the region around 2,600 years ago.

PLUMPTON HALL - in 1856 a hoard of about 1000 coins was found in a red-brown coloured jar around 18 inches high and 10 inches wide at the middle, but narrowing at neck and foot. The coins were of Gal Menus (AD 260–69), Marius (AD 268), Salonina (AD 268), Victorinus (AD 269–71), Tericus (AD 261–73), Claudius Gothicus (AD 268–70), Aurelian (AD 270–75) and Probus (AD 276–82)

CASTLEMERE HOARD - discovered in 1896, the hoard contained a sizeable number of coins dating to the reign of Emperor Claudius (AD 41–59). It may have been deposited during the tribal war which precipitated the Roman intervention in the north of Britain

STUBLEY HALL, LITTLEBOROUGH - in the early 19th century an 'urn containing Roman coins, and a Roman cup' were found

TOWN HOUSE, LITTLEBOROUGH - in 1883 Roman coins and tiles were found

BLACKSTONE EDGE - during surveying work in 1889 a nine-inch long iron spearhead thought to be Roman was recovered.
In 1926 two coins of Vespasian (AD 69–79) were collected

HOLLINGWOOD BROOK, NEAR CLEGGS WOOD - in 1994 metal detectorists unearthed a hoard of 65 silver coins deposited between AD 192 and 222

Top: Bronze torc found at Mowroad, Calderbrook in 1832 (courtesy of Touchstones Rochdale)

Centre: Roman finds in the Rochdale area

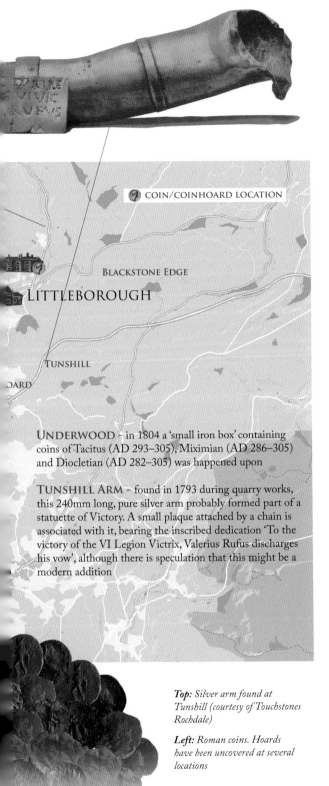

BLACKSTONE EDGE

LITTLEBOROUGH

TUNSHILL

OARD

UNDERWOOD - in 1804 a 'small iron box' containing coins of Tacitus (AD 293–305), Miximian (AD 286–305) and Diocletian (AD 282–305) was happened upon

TUNSHILL ARM - found in 1793 during quarry works, this 240mm long, pure silver arm probably formed part of a statuette of Victory. A small plaque attached by a chain is associated with it, bearing the inscribed dedication 'To the victory of the VI Legion Victrix, Valerius Rufus discharges his vow', although there is speculation that this might be a modern addition

Top: *Silver arm found at Tunshill (courtesy of Touchstones Rochdale)*

Left: *Roman coins. Hoards have been uncovered at several locations*

Although the lowland areas along the River Roch would have been attractive to prehistoric communities, archaeological evidence of Iron Age occupation, such as field systems or hut circles, is lacking. Rather than suggesting a lack of occupation, however, this paucity of evidence can likely be attributed to the destruction of archaeological remains by later, industrial-era development, which was concentrated in the river valley.

By the late Iron Age, the north and north-west of modern-day England were controlled by the Brigantes, a tribal political entity made up of several sub-tribes. The Roman conquest of southern Britain in the mid-1st century AD destabilised the political equilibrium within Brigantian society, resulting in a civil war between the different sub-tribes. By AD 70 the Roman general Agricola's intervention in the civil war had led to the Roman occupation of the Brigantes territory, including the area now covered by Rochdale. Roman occupation across what is now Greater Manchester is well attested and was focused on the Roman forts at Manchester, Castleshaw and Wigan.

Many Roman-era artefacts were found by chance: therefore often a complete account of an artefact's origin or the precise circumstances of its discovery have not been recorded. Despite the presence of some Roman finds in the Rochdale area, no Roman settlement sites are known beyond those connected to the forts. Again, rather than indicating a lack of occupation, the intensity and extent of industrial development in Rochdale has likely removed evidence of Roman settlement.

Medieval Rochdale

In the territory stretching from Hadrian's Wall to the River Mersey and Humber Estuary, the Roman system of civil and military administration was upheld by the Duke of the Britains (*Dux Britanniarum*) until around AD 500. At this time the region was divided, with the western portion (Lancashire and Cumbria) creating the Celtic Kingdom of Reged. Rochdale probably held some significance as it was situated at the convergence of three routes through the Pennines.

Archaeological evidence for the Kingdom of Rheged and its subsequent incorporation into Saxon Northumberland is completely lacking. However, it was probably during this period of Northumbrian control that the Hundred of Salford was established, with the parish of Rochdale forming the largest parish within it.

The earliest reference to Rochdale is in the Domesday Book of 1086, which lists 'Recedham', meaning 'homestead with a hall' or 'village of the people of Rheged'. The name of the river 'Roch' (formerly spelt 'Roach') was derived from this name for the town.

During Edward the Confessor's reign (1042–66), Rochdale is listed as one of the holdings of Gamel the Thane, one of 21 men holding land in the Manor of Radcliffe granted to them by the king. After the Norman Conquest in 1066, Gamel seems to have held on to Rochdale even though the Hundred of Salford, which included the Manor of Radcliffe, was part of the lands given to a Norman called Roger de Poitou.

Above: Map showing Kingdom of Rheged and Northumbria. Rheged was established earlier than Northumbria and eventually made up part of the kingdom

Opposite

Left: Timeline, featuring coats of arms of some of the families *Top: The Lacy arms* *Middle: Arms of Henry Grosmont, 1st Duke of Lancaster (© Sodacan)* *Bottom: Byron arms*

Right: Index map to the Parish of Rochdale

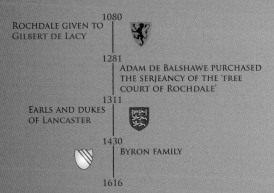

1080
ROCHDALE GIVEN TO
GILBERT DE LACY

1281
ADAM DE BALSHAWE PURCHASED
THE SERJEANCY OF THE 'FREE
COURT OF ROCHDALE'

1311
EARLS AND DUKES
OF LANCASTER

1430
BYRON FAMILY

1616

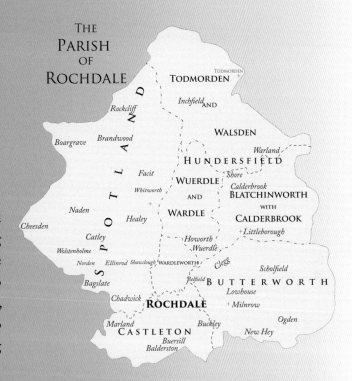

THE
PARISH
OF
ROCHDALE

Documentary sources suggest that in around 1195 the town was renamed 'Rachedal', meaning 'valley of the River Roch'. The parish of Rochdale covered over 41,000 acres and extended north to Bacup and Todmorden (now in West Yorkshire), and from the Cheesden Valley in the west to Saddleworth in the east, with Rochdale being located close to the parish's southern boundary.

 As the climate and geography of Rochdale were unfavourable for widespread arable agriculture, pastoral farming must have dominated the local economy. However, grain production was not completely absent as was evidenced by several corn mills utilising the abundant fast-flowing watercourses in the area. Therefore, medieval Rochdale probably comprised dispersed clusters of dwellings spread across agricultural land. Settlement in the town until the early 13th century was probably focused on the castle, but may have moved closer to the parish church and the crossing point over the River Roch thereafter.

During the 13th century, increased internal and external trading led to the expansion of England's economy and the concurrent granting of Royal Charters to hold markets and fairs. Although an unchartered market was likely held in Rochdale from the early 12th century, Edmund de Lacy was granted a Royal Charter in 1251 to hold a weekly market on Wednesdays, along with an annual fair during the feast of St Simon and St Jude on 28th October. It has been suggested that the original marketplace was located in Church Stile, near the parish church, although confirmation awaits further archaeological investigation.

Norman settlement in Rochdale is represented by the site of a motte and bailey castle thought to have stood at the northern end of Castle Hill, half a mile to the south-west of St Chad's Church. The castle was surveyed in 1823 during the construction of the Manchester to Rochdale turnpike road. In 1889, a reproduction of the resultant plan was published in *The History of the Parish of Rochdale in the County of Lancaster*, written by local historian and twice Mayor of Rochdale, Henry Fishwick (1835–1914).

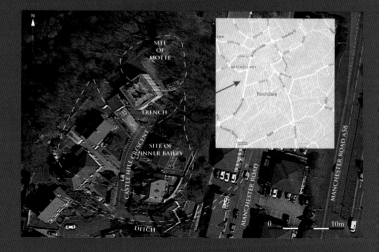

On the plan, it can be seen that the mound, or motte, was flat-topped and stood at the apex of the triangular Castle Hill. The bailey, a fortified enclosure, was located to the south of the mound and was an irregular square shape. The motte and bailey were surrounded by an earth rampart and ditch, with a second ditch added to the south and south-east. A timber wall was likely constructed on top of the earthen rampart. The castle features in 12th-century charters but is not mentioned again until the 17th century, suggesting it was abandoned in the early 13th century. Its earthworks were levelled when Castle Hill House was constructed in the 1820s. In 1983, during the construction of new housing at Castle Hill, the Greater Manchester Archaeological Unit excavated several trenches on the presumed edge of the outer bailey. Unfortunately, no medieval artefacts were discovered.

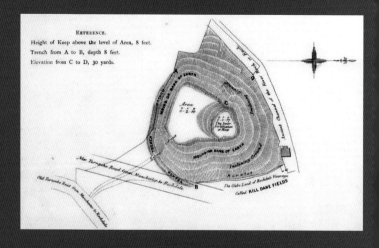

During renovation of Castle Hill House in 2001, the Greater Manchester Archaeological Unit conducted an archaeological evaluation. This consisted of the excavation of a 5m x 1m trench across the lawn opposite the house's entrance. Additionally, two 1m square test pits were excavated to the north and east of the house.

Due to their limited size, none of the trenches extended beyond a depth of around 1m below ground level. Consequently, only 19th-century levelling layers were exposed. These layers, which contained fragments of brick and pottery, were probably deposited during the construction of Castle Hill House.

It was concluded that features evidencing medieval occupation, such as post holes, pits and hearths, had probably been removed by 19th-century landscaping, which appears to have reduced the level of the motte. However, a sherd of medieval pottery was recovered from the motte area during construction groundworks, confirming medieval occupation at the site.

Opposite

Top: *Outline of Rochdale Castle superimposed on modern satellite imagery (© Google)*

Middle: *The Greater Manchester Archaeological Unit excavation at Castle Hill House in 1983 (courtesy of GMAAS)*

Bottom: *A detailed plan of Rochdale Castle reproduced in Henry Fishwick's 1889 History of Rochdale*

This page

Above: *Photograph of the 1m x 5m trench excavated in 2001 (courtesy of GMAAS)*

Right: *Photograph showing the location of the trench in relation to Castle Hill House (courtesy of GMAAS)*

The increasing demand for wool in the 14th century appears to have caused a shift from cattle- to sheep-rearing in the Rochdale area, and Rochdale had become a well-established market centre by the 15th century, supplied by satellite hamlets where the wool was processed. The movement of wool between small producers on the periphery and the market in Rochdale was undertaken on a network of trackways. Two examples of probable medieval routeways located in the south-east of the borough – Moss Side Lane and Moor Bank Lane – were investigated during the Kingsway Business Park development in 2004–05. The routeways consisted of two raised earthen banks on either side of a sunken hollowed-out trackway.

Although the parish church of Rochdale is not mentioned in the Domesday Book, it is thought that a church may have stood on the hill overlooking the town since the late 7th century, a conclusion drawn circumstantially from the church's dedication to St Chad – the Bishop of Mercia in AD 673. In 1903, during repairs to the north-west part of the churchyard's wall, Dr Wilson, the vicar, identified a partially buried wall formed from slates of Whitworth stone, which were interpreted as pre-Norman in date.

If there was an earlier parish church, it was likely rebuilt after the Norman Conquest. Fragments of masonry dating to the Norman period are said to have been discovered during building works in the church in 1816, including a zigzag moulding considered to be part of a door arch and a rounded stone thought to be a font. Additionally, a tear-shaped bottle believed to be Roman was discovered in the church's Trinity Chapel.

The earliest documentary evidence of a church at Rochdale dates to around 1170 when Adam de Spotland granted land to the Church of St Chad. A half-pillar of 13th-century date represents the oldest visible masonry in the church. The founding of a parish church in Rochdale at this time suggests that the population in the parish was growing, a situation supported by agricultural labour intensification, greater food production, and consequently increased tax revenues, which were invested into institutions such as the church.

In the mid-14th century, the Black Death greatly reduced the population and destabilised the complex economic and social systems that had developed in the preceding centuries. However, the economy did gradually recover and by the 15th century Rochdale had become a well-established market centre once again, predominantly dealing in woollen goods. The increasing wealth generated by the expanding woollen trade was reflected in investment in the fabric of St Chad's Church. For example, in 1558 the nave arcade was rebuilt with Perpendicular arches, whilst in the 15th century a new chapel, Trinity Chapel, was constructed within the church building.

Opposite

Above: *Moor Bank Lane (© Oxford Archaeology)*

Below: *Moss Side Lane (© Oxford Archaeology)*

This page

Top: *An illustration showing the nave of St Chad's Church before the renovations of 1853. The 16th-century Perpendicular arches of the nave arcade can be seen to the left (courtesy of Touchstones Rochdale)*

Bottom: *The south porch of St Chad's prior to renovation in 1873 (courtesy of Touchstones Rochdale)*

POST-MEDIEVAL ROCHDALE

The concept of the post-medieval period, as differentiated from the preceding medieval period, is a simple way to bracket the complex and wide-ranging political, economic and social changes that resulted in the events of the 16th, 17th and early 18th centuries. In the case of Rochdale, the overarching character of the economy, and to an extent its social and political life, was a continuation of the structures established in the late medieval period. As discussed, increasing demand for wool compelled a shift from cattle-rearing to sheep-raising and thus the production of wool was already an important part of the local economy by the 16th century. Wool was processed at a domestic scale in satellite hamlets, while Rochdale served as a market centre where goods were traded, and cloth was processed in the water-powered fulling mills positioned on the banks of the Roch. Many of the farms that would be rebuilt in the early 17th century with proceeds from the woollen trade had their origins in the medieval period. Another example of continuity was the persistent presence of many of the influential families from the medieval era, including the Byrons, Asshetons and Savilles, throughout successive centuries.

The Reformation and the associated Dissolution of the Monasteries during the 1530s may be taken to represent the key events that signalled the onset of the post-medieval period. In 1537 the dissolving of Whalley Abbey, a wealthy Cistercian house, resulted in the redistribution of extensive agricultural land in Rochdale parish – previously held by the Church – to loyal supporters of the Crown such as at Spotland Manor, which was granted to the Holt dynasty. Religious foundations were taken into the Crown's control and in 1547 the right to appoint vicars, and to appropriate the revenues generated from ecclesiastical taxes, was granted to the Archbishop of Canterbury.

Extract from Saxton's map of 1577, showing the main settlements in the region

An upturn in demand for woollen products stimulated by expanding internal and external trade during the 16th century brought wealth to the region that was manifested in Rochdale with the founding of new buildings and institutions. This included the installation, in 1552, of an organ in St Chad's Church (one of only two in Lancashire), and the rebuilding of the church's nave in 1558. A grammar school was constructed in Rochdale in 1565, and in 1566 a deputy Aulnager – an official representative for the inspection and taxation of woollen goods – was commissioned. Another indicator of growing prosperity, underpinned mainly by the growth in the woollen trade, was the building and rebuilding of many yeoman tenant farms and the halls of the gentry in the rural hinterland of Rochdale in the early 17th century. Examples include Dearnley Old Hall and Clegg Hall, both in Littleborough, and Newbold Hall in Rochdale, which was excavated by the Centre for Applied Archaeology in 2010.

Given that Newbold Hall is referenced in the Coucher Book of Whalley (1199–1216), the hall likely had its origins as a medieval manorial seat. No vestiges of a medieval building were revealed during the 2010 excavation the earliest remains exposed being the early 17th-century stone-built foundations of an L-shaped building. This likely suggests that the original manor house was sited outside of the excavation area. In the post-medieval period, it wasn't unusual for old manor houses to be demolished and replaced with new halls nearby.

Not a great deal is known about the inhabitants of Newbold Hall but a document from 1620 states that Edward Newbold died there and at that time the Newbold estate was held by Sir John Byron. A lease from 1627 relates that Newbold Hall was owned by Richard Schofield; the hall was sold to Thomas Hindley in 1707.

Research into the post-medieval manor houses of north-west England has determined a three-tiered categorisation of halls based on their size. These categories correspond to the three social groups – tenant, freeholder and lord – that occupied the upper parts of the social hierarchy. Newbold Hall's size and structural form are characteristic of the middle, freeholder, tier of halls. Freeholder halls often featured an arrangement of buildings characterised by a hall with one or two cross wings, generating either an L-shaped or an H-shaped plan.

The excavation revealed that two side wings were added to the structure in the later part of the 17th century. These additions produced a layout which mimicked the forms of the largest halls in the region, which all had a central open hall, with ranges of two-storey buildings set around open courtyards. Land and wealth were redistributed during the mid-16th century as a result of the Reformation and the consequent reorganisation of government and the ruling elite. Consequently, there was an expansion of the freeholder class. Along with these social changes, domestic structures rebuilt in the 16th and 17th centuries demonstrate a fundamentally different approach to the way that earlier high-status buildings were organised and arranged. The display of social status was reflected in the use of new architectural styles and materials.

While late medieval great houses often had a defensive appearance that typically included a moat and an inward-looking layout, the design of post-medieval manor houses commonly favoured symmetrical, elaborately decorated façades and outward-facing building arrangements. The communal layout of medieval great houses, which was centred around the great hall, was replaced with more private spaces such as inglenook fireplaces and private dining rooms. Essentially, post-medieval houses were arranged to increase social segregation between the family and the servants. This was matched with specialised room functions and an increase in house size, allowing greater personal space.

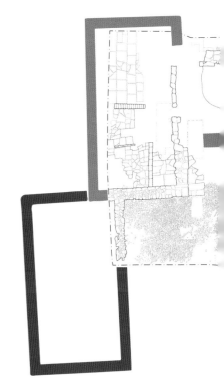

Top: Plan of the excavated remains of Newbold Hall. Lighter brown walls are early 17th century, darker brown walls are late 17th century (© University of Salford)

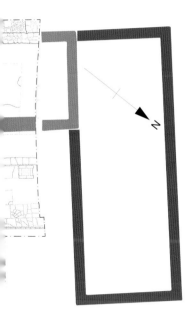

EWBOLD STREET

0   10 m

Bottom: Aerial view of the site, looking north (© University of Salford)

The results of the excavation suggested that the hall's northern wing was demolished and rebuilt *c.* 1800. Later additions that included partition walls and flagstone flooring were associated with the remodelling of the hall's interior in the period between *c.* 1844 and 1900 when it was used as a public house.

Supporting the agricultural economy of Rochdale were two water-powered corn mills in the centre of the town, Rochdale Mill and Town Mill. These mills likely occupied the sites of medieval corn mills. By 1626, there was also a horse-powered malt-grinding mill located near the market, and a fulling mill is also known to have been located near Town Mill for processing woollen cloth. This was just one of several fulling mills, another being Oakenrod Mill, which was evaluated archaeologically by Oxford Archaeology North in 2006. This initial investigation of the site uncovered substantial remains of the mill, including two well-preserved head-race tunnels that connected with an intact waterwheel pit and a later turbine pit.

By the early 17th century Rochdale had developed into an important regional market town serving the farming community, and was also a focus for the burgeoning textile trade. In the sparsely populated areas around Rochdale, income created by spinning and weaving wool increasingly supplemented the subsistence agriculture practised on isolated family farms. As the rural economy became more reliant on the production and processing of woollen goods, many farms began to dedicate rooms to textile production.

Pits containing decomposed textile waste were found during excavations Oxford Archaeology North conducted at the locations of former 17th-century farmhouses at the Kingsway Business Park. The archaeological evidence was enhanced by documentary sources that confirm the inhabitants of the farms were clothmakers. John Milne who occupied Near Moor Bank Farm, for example, was an important woollen clothier who, in 1664, also became a woollen merchant.

In addition to wool production and subsistence agriculture, some small-scale coal mining had probably taken place in the area since the late medieval period. A coal pit at Knowle House near Littleborough was documented as early as 1580. The negative impact that mining had on the landscape was commented on in 1626 when a female collier, Alice Wolstanholme, is noted disapprovingly as having cut down many trees when 'supplying of her pits' at Wardle. However, the coal industry was never as important in Rochdale as in other parts of south Lancashire.

A survey of the manor was commissioned by Sir Robert Heath in 1626, which also provides a description of Rochdale during this period. The survey states that the land located between Castle Hill and Molesworth Street, south of the river, was owned by the Church; and the cattle market was held on the old medieval market site near Church Lane. The only buildings located on the Church lands in 1626 were seven small houses or farms, six houses in Church Lane, the church, the vicarage and the grammar school. However, further houses were built on these lands as the century progressed, particularly on Church Lane and Packer Street. The church steps between Packer Street and the church were also rebuilt around 1660. By the early 1640s, the population of the parish is thought to have risen to around 10,000 people. The town was assessed in 1666 under the Hearth Tax. This assessment showed that all of the 14 men assessed besides one, the vicar, were woollen manufacturers or merchants.

Below: The head of the old market cross, which was broken off in the 1770s and is now on display in the town museum

The political and religious sympathies of those in the Rochdale area were split between the Parliamentarian and Royalist causes during the Civil War (1642–51). Many of the local gentry were Royalists, such as Sir John Byron, who was made commander of the King's forces in Lancashire and Cheshire, and was created Baron Byron in 1643 in recognition of his services to King Charles I. Byron was declared a rebel by Parliament in 1651. No military engagements occurred in Rochdale, although Colonel John Rosworm placed a garrison of 1,200 in Rochdale and 800 more on Blackstone Edge to protect the town from Royalist forces led by the Earl of Newcastle. Sir Ralph Assheton, a local lord of the manor, fought several battles against the King's forces during the Civil War. Also during the 17th century, a series of vicars of Rochdale took a puritanical standpoint and in 1662, the vicar Robert Bathe refused to conform to the Act of Uniformity and was removed from his post.

Above: Extract from a plan of the vicarage lands, dating to 1764, showing what pre-industrial Rochdale was like

Below: Grammar School, Rochdale, Lancashire: children playing in the front. Tinted lithograph by J.K. Colling after J. Clarke (Wellcome Collection. Public Domain Mark)

The continuing expansion of the market for wool during the early 18th century compelled tenant farmers to reinvest capital into the construction of two- and three-storey weavers' workshops, where the artisanal production of woollen goods could be intensified. Merchants erected homes and warehouses in Rochdale, and commercial enterprises such as inns sprung up to service the tradesmen. Such buildings were concentrated along Yorkshire Street and associated side roads on the north side of the River Roch, and along Packer Street and Church Lane to the south of Rochdale Bridge. Fine examples of buildings from this period include the Union Flag Hotel (now Lloyd's Bank), Yates's Wine Lodge and the Wellington Hotel, and their presence in Rochdale represents the ever-growing wealth of the Georgian town. The construction of these buildings effectively relocated the town's centre to the north bank of the river, where a 'new' town was established.

A notable constraint to the expansion of the woollen trade was the poor-quality transport infrastructure in the Rochdale area, which until the mid-18th century consisted solely of a road network that had not been considerably improved since the departure of the Romans. Throughout the winter and frequently for much of the rest of the year, the majority of these roads were not fit for wheeled transportation. Locally, woollen products were transported to and from the surrounding farmsteads and further afield via a network of packhorse trails that were often paved with flagstones. Although improvements to roads began to be made with the introduction of turnpike trusts in the mid-18th century, it was appreciated that a new form of transportation, namely canals, would need to be brought to Rochdale if the desired increases in manufacturing and trade, and therefore wealth, were to be realised.

ROCHDALE CANAL AND CANAL BASIN

In 1698 a petition requesting that the rivers Aire and Calder be made navigable was signed by the clothiers of Rochdale. The petition sparked a wave of interest in providing a navigable waterway through Rochdale and the surrounding areas to serve the growing industries. Indeed, the arrival of a canal in Rochdale 100 years later would be a significant impetus for industrial expansion.

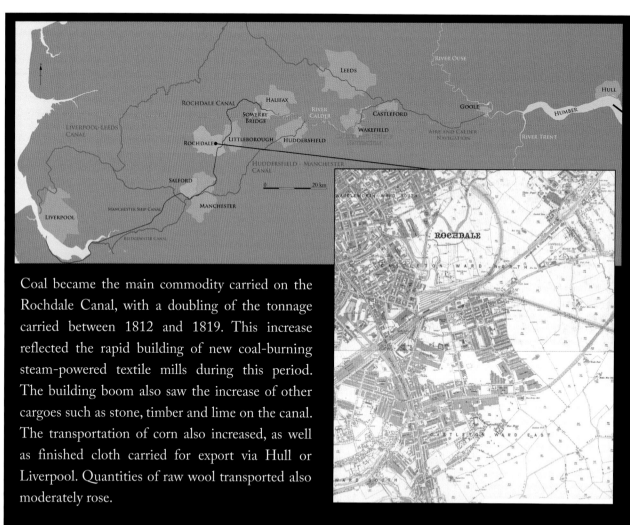

Coal became the main commodity carried on the Rochdale Canal, with a doubling of the tonnage carried between 1812 and 1819. This increase reflected the rapid building of new coal-burning steam-powered textile mills during this period. The building boom also saw the increase of other cargoes such as stone, timber and lime on the canal. The transportation of corn also increased, as well as finished cloth carried for export via Hull or Liverpool. Quantities of raw wool transported also moderately rose.

Top: Route of the Rochdale Canal

Right: The Rochdale Canal shown on the 25-inch to the mile Ordnance Survey map. Surveyed 1889–91. Published in 1893

Opposite: An early 20th-century, north-east looking view of the eastern arm of the Drake Street canal basin with the wharf warehouse to the left of the basin arm and Vicars Moss Mill to the right (courtesy of Touchstones Rochdale)

The canal was authorised by an Act of Parliament on 4 April 1794, which created the Rochdale Canal Company (RCC) and sanctioned the building of a canal across the Pennines from Sowerby Bridge – where it would join the Calder and Hebble Navigation – to Manchester, eventually connecting with the Bridgewater Canal. A canal across the Pennines would allow the effective supply of coal to industries along its route and facilitate the transportation of goods produced in mills to the ports of Hull and Liverpool. This was the first canal to be opened over the difficult-to-navigate terrain of the South Pennines. The route chosen was not the most direct but it eschewed the need for a tunnel between the Calder and Rochdale valleys by traversing the upland pass lying between Littleborough and Todmorden. Construction of the whole canal would take around 13 years and cost £600,000, but sections were opened as and when they were completed. The Rochdale Branch, which was about half a mile (0.8km) long, was the first to open, in 1798, from a basin at Drake Street to the main line of the canal. The basin served as an inland port for Rochdale and was essential to the town's trade. In 1845, when the usage of the canal peaked, almost a million tonnes of cargo was transported and this amount consistently remained at around 800,000 tonnes until the beginning of the 20th century.

The exact date at which the canal basin was constructed is unclear, although it was certainly open by 1804. The location chosen by the RCC to build its basin was practical and well-considered. Lying as close to the town centre as the topography permitted, the canal basin consisted of two arms flanking a central wharf.

The opening of the canal and the basin stimulated the development of Drake Street and fed into the continuing expansion of Rochdale as an industrial centre. This was because water transportation enabled raw materials and finished products to be imported and exported more efficiently than road transportation, facilitating economic growth. Commodities and raw materials were shipped between Yorkshire and Lancashire, and to or from the international ports of Liverpool and Hull.

The basins were surrounded by wharves where goods such as coal, stone and timber were stockpiled, and by warehouses that accommodated storage for either outgoing or incoming perishable goods such as cotton, flour, paper and grain. A pent roof extended from the face of the western warehouse to cover the loading and offloading of goods from barges within the basin. A brick-built stanchion that would have supported the roof was exposed during an archaeological investigation of the canal basin carried out by Museum of London Archaeology (MOLA) in 2022–23. The foundations of the eastern warehouse, which had two internal boat holes where cargo was hoisted from barges, were also uncovered.

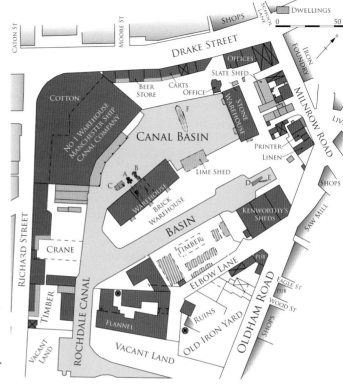

Above: *Rochdale Canal Basin in 1900 based on Charles Goad's Insurance Plan, which provided detailed information used to assess the fire risk of urban buildings. Six canal barges are shown on the plan; these were excavated by MOLA in 2022 (A, B, C, D, E and F)*

Below: *One of the canal wharf warehouses stands derelict c. 1970s (courtesy of Touchstones Rochdale)*

The Manchester to Leeds Railway, which served Rochdale from 1839, offered the many industries in the town an even more efficient means of transportation for goods to areas throughout the country and abroad. Following the advent of the railway, the amount of cargo transported on the canal began to decline, although it was not until after the First World War that the canal became economically unviable. The last complete journey along the Rochdale Canal was made in 1937, and an Act of Parliament was obtained in 1952 to ban public navigation. The Drake Street basin was infilled during the 1970s and the site repurposed as the Central Retail Park.

The excavation of the basin in 2022–23 exposed the partial remains of six vessels that had been deliberately abandoned by the Rochdale Canal Company in June 1921 when the company disbanded and sold the fleet. Three of the vessels were Mersey flat-type boats – a distinctive double-ended, carvel-built barge typical of the North West region that was capable of plying the tidal Mersey and had a relatively high cargo carrying capacity of 60 to 90 tonnes, even with the shallow draught (4ft) of the Rochdale Canal. These sorts of vessels were produced across the region in the yards of companies such as Rathbone's in Stretford and Yarwood's in Northwich. The excavated boats were likely built in the mid-19th century and were therefore around 50 to 100 years old when they were abandoned. None of the vessels had nameplates attached as they had probably been removed as mementoes. However, documentary sources provide the names of three of the vessels: *Rose*, *Foxglove* and *Holly* (or *Henry*). As well as the Mersey flats, a pontoon or float was discovered. The hull of this vessel was packed with bricks and Portland cement that was likely used as ballast and provided a flat surface to work on.

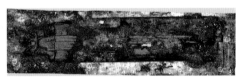

Far left: The stern of a 72ft-long Mersey flat-type barge exposed during the excavation (courtesy of MOLA)

Left: Canal Barges A, B and F. Scan the code to view 3D models, created by MOLA

At the turn of the 19th century, Rochdale's economy was booming. The canal afforded more efficient transportation of raw materials and products than previously, and the advent of new spinning technologies, such as Arkwright's water frame and the spinning mule, introduced in the late 18th century, facilitated the emergence of cotton as a viable financial enterprise. To take advantage of the region's expanding textile industry, enterprising mill owners established mills along Rochdale's abundant smaller streams and rivers. In 1784 the water frame had been adapted to spin wool, although it was not until the introduction of the fully automatic mule run by steam power in the 1820s that mechanised wool spinning became common. The advent of steam-powered factories meant mills no longer needed to be built in locations where waterwheels could be driven, although access to water was still a requisite for running steam-powered technologies. Whilst the production of cotton goods began to gain a foothold in the local economy, the woollen industry remained an important component, with a focus in particular on the production of flannel and baize.

With the establishment of new textile mills came the emergence of numerous associated industries. These included warehousing businesses, firms supplying machinery, and other more general engineering works. Warehouses in Rochdale were clustered around the canal terminus and railway goods station and were dotted in amongst mills in other parts of the town, for example at Robert Street where a small mid-19th-century warehouse had developed from an earlier coach house, or on Smith Street where large purpose-built warehouses were situated. Foundries, where tools, parts and machinery were manufactured, could also be found scattered across the town with examples including the Roch Brass and Iron Foundry, built south of the river behind Packer Street, and the Wellington Foundry, situated in River Street, which was investigated archaeologically by Oxford Archaeology North. Other subsidiary industries were also established next to the Roch, the waters of which were considered clean enough to service bleaching, printing and dyeing works. Another trade bolstered by the increasing mechanisation within mills was the tanning industry, and Salford Archaeology investigated a 19th-century tannery located on Kitchen Street, to the east of the town centre.

Also around the turn of the 19th century, dedicated housing for industrial workers in the form of two-storey back-to-back terraces began to be constructed in Rochdale by property speculators eager to maximise the potential of available building space. Since less material was needed for walls and roofs than in detached buildings, terraced houses were less expensive to construct. Due to transport infrastructure being limited at this time, workers' housing was usually located close to people's places of work. This was the case in Rochdale where examples of early 19th-century housing – investigated archaeologically by Salford Archaeology on the Rochdale Riverside redevelopment sites – stood close to Butts, Duncan Street and Bowling Green Mills.

At first, as there was little legislative control and a premium for space, industrial housing could be overcrowded, poorly lit and unventilated, although in the case of Rochdale dwellings seem to have been of higher quality than those in Salford and Manchester. As local bye-laws were introduced from the mid-19th century onwards housing conditions came to be regulated with stipulations for the provision of outside toilets, the minimum sizes of backyards, ceiling heights and a minimum size of windows.

Top: Textile mills on Smith Street c. 1926 (courtesy of Touchstones Rochdale)

Bottom: Butts Mill, a steam-powered woollen mill on Smith Street in the centre of Rochdale, prior to 1904 (courtesy of Touchstones Rochdale)

A defining feature of the industrial landscape was the railway. The line linking Manchester with Leeds was constructed between 1837 and 1841, with a station built at Rochdale in 1839. Like the canals, only more so, railways were instrumental as an enabler for developing industries because they allowed raw materials and goods to be transported more cheaply and quickly than before.

By the mid-19th century, with the rising population and the wealth generated by the booming industries, new civic, social and commercial infrastructures were established in industrialised areas. This included the foundation of many new churches, which tended to be associated with Nonconformist denominations that appealed more to the working class than the Church of England, and also because Rochdale was traditionally staunchly Protestant and generally liberal.

The oldest Nonconformist chapel in Rochdale was the Unitarian Chapel on Blackwater Street, built in 1690. Other Nonconformist buildings constructed in the town during the 19th century included a United Presbyterian church, a Baptist chapel, a Quaker meeting house, a Wesleyan chapel, two Unitarian chapels and other independent chapels. Many of these chapels were demolished in the 20th century and have been understood from archive sources or archaeological survey or excavation.

Above: An example of a works building on the east side of Acker Street, photographed in 1970 (courtesy of Touchstones Rochdale)

Below: Mid-19th-century two-up, two-down terraced housing with cellars on Portland Street, 1971 (courtesy of Touchstones Rochdale)

Recent examples of archaeologically excavated Nonconformist chapels include Milton Street Congregational Church and the Church of the Good Shepherd on the corner of Kitchen Street and Ramsey Street. Two examples of extant Nonconformist buildings that have been subjected to detailed standing building recording surveys are a Baptist chapel on Harriet Street and a Presbyterian chapel on Smith Street.

Above: Rochdale Smith Street Primitive Methodist Chapel. According to Past and Present Methodist Chapels, the building belonged to the Christian Science Church when it closed in 1980 (from the collection of Rev Steven Wild)

Below: Photograph of 13 of the original members of the Rochdale Society of Equitable Pioneers

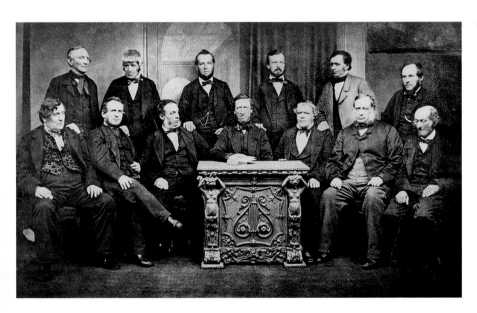

Other social institutions were established to attempt to rectify the overwhelmingly poor social and economic conditions suffered by the industrial working classes – a result of the unregulated capitalism that had developed in conjunction with industrialisation. A salient example is the Rochdale Society of Equitable Pioneers, set up in 1844 to counter the poor-quality housing and food provided by factory owners.

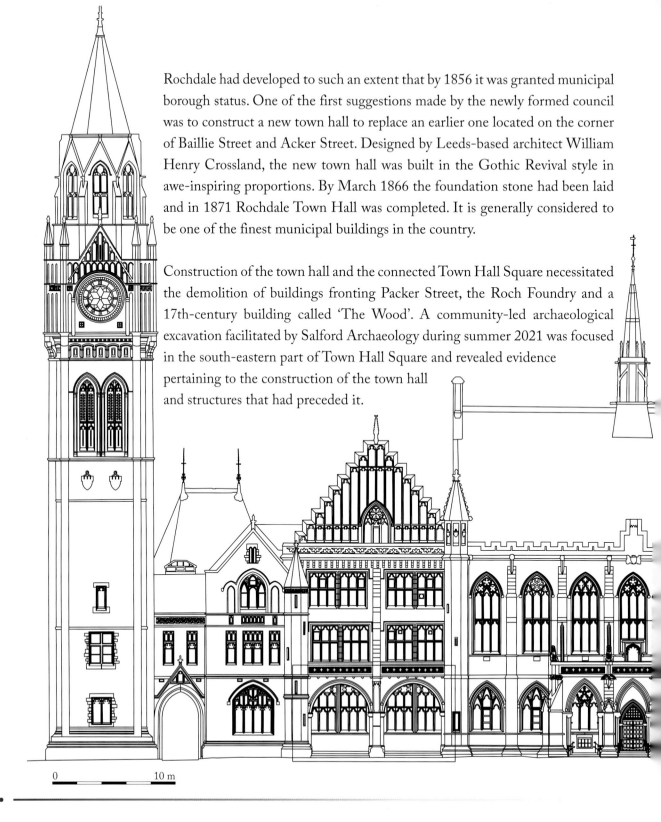

Rochdale had developed to such an extent that by 1856 it was granted municipal borough status. One of the first suggestions made by the newly formed council was to construct a new town hall to replace an earlier one located on the corner of Baillie Street and Acker Street. Designed by Leeds-based architect William Henry Crossland, the new town hall was built in the Gothic Revival style in awe-inspiring proportions. By March 1866 the foundation stone had been laid and in 1871 Rochdale Town Hall was completed. It is generally considered to be one of the finest municipal buildings in the country.

Construction of the town hall and the connected Town Hall Square necessitated the demolition of buildings fronting Packer Street, the Roch Foundry and a 17th-century building called 'The Wood'. A community-led archaeological excavation facilitated by Salford Archaeology during summer 2021 was focused in the south-eastern part of Town Hall Square and revealed evidence pertaining to the construction of the town hall and structures that had preceded it.

0   10 m

Lancashire's cotton mills and their textile workers were almost completely reliant on the labour of three million enslaved cotton pickers in the American Deep South. During the 1860s, when cotton shipments were blocked during the American Civil War, Rochdale experienced a 'Golden Age' spurred by rising demand for the woollen products that were still produced in the town. The local economy boomed, as reflected in a 60% increase in Rochdale's population in the 1860s. However, by the 1870s cotton spinning once again became the dominant industry in the borough.

Civic institutions continued to be established throughout the 19th century with new fire and police stations built. Other examples include Smith Street public baths, built in 1868, and schools like those on Baillie Street and Penn Street. Libraries, galleries, hospitals and cemeteries were also established in the second half of the 19th century, and Rochdale's transport infrastructure was greatly improved with the installation of a tram network. By the late 19th century, the social institutions highlighted above were complemented by an array of commercial premises that had sprung up in the centre of Rochdale and along its main thoroughfares, representing physical expressions of industrialised consumption, which continues to have an enormous influence on the social structure and economy of Britain.

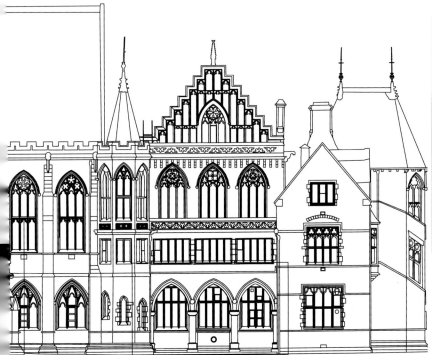

Above: The Leica RTC360 was one of the 3D scanners used in recording the town hall (courtesy of Steven Tamburello)

Left: Measured drawing of the front elevation of Rochdale Town Hall (© University of Salford)

River Street Iron Works

By the late 18th century, the burgeoning textile industry was driving the rapid evolution of factories, resulting in a growing demand for machinery, steam engines, boilers, gearing and a wide range of other iron goods. Initially, individual components of the machinery were built by tradespeople including millwrights, mechanics, blacksmiths and joiners, but increasing demand and complexity of the machinery led to the appearance of specialised engineering works to serve the textile industry.

A relatively early example of an engineering works was investigated in 2007 by Oxford Archaeology North ahead of constructing a new transport interchange at River Street. An assessment of historic documents and maps concluded that there was potential for the survival of the buried remains of an early 19th-century iron foundry that had been associated with the Petrie family, who rose to prominence as a leading supplier of machinery to the textile industry. This inference was confirmed by evaluation trenching, which exposed well-preserved foundations of 19th-century industrial buildings.

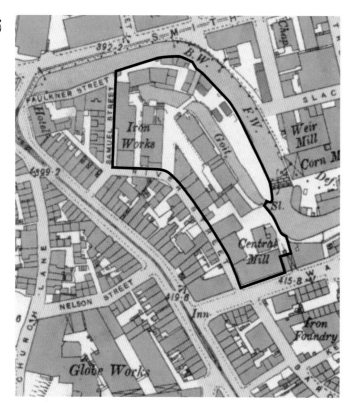

The Petries

The engineering works on River Street were occupied by John Petrie, a manufacturer of textile machinery. John came from a family of ironworkers and engineers. His father, Alexander, had migrated to Bury in 1793 from Scotland and established a foundry where he and his sons worked.

Opposite: River Street site location superimposed on the 25-inch Ordnance Survey map, published in 1893, along with images of the foundry (courtesy of Oxford Archaeology)

Above: Petrie's Harrow Wool Scourer

Below: Advertisements taken out by the Petries in Worralls Comerical Directory of Lancashire for 1879

As the textile industry grew in north-west England, demand for machinery parts increased and it was decided that the eldest son, John, should set up a branch foundry in Rochdale to capitalise on growing trade. John's first foundry, which came into production in 1814, was within a row of converted cottages on Cheetham Street. The Rochdale enterprise proved more profitable than the Bury one, which was closed and new premises – the Phoenix Foundry on Whitehall Street – completed in 1816. Initially the firm's business was concerned with the production of small castings for textile machinery, but in 1819 Petrie manufactured an entire beam engine, becoming the first steam-engine maker in Rochdale. This was probably built in the newly established River Street foundry.

Alexander Petrie died in 1823 and John Petrie became the head of the company. John was greatly influenced by his father, who made much of his identity as a Scot: he had lived simply and frugally, apparently eating porridge every morning, and cherished his Scottish accent. John Petrie was a religious man; he was dour, proud and stubborn, and kept a tight hold on the company's direction and purse strings. John restricted the firm's output to the production of simple, single-expansion beam engines that worked at low steam pressures. Consequently, they gained a reputation for reliable but conservative and relatively heavy engine designs.

John's son, John Petrie Junior, formed his own engineering enterprise and in 1853 patented and made the first automatic wool-washing machine, in a workshop in Church Lane. Due to increased demand, his company was able to expand to the River Street Iron Works. In 1920, John Petrie Jnr Ltd amalgamated with rival Rochdale engineering company J & W McNaught. The new company took the title of Petrie & McNaught Ltd and continued to manufacture machinery until the 1960s.

JOHN PETRIE,
WHOLESALE AND RETAIL
MILL AND FURNISHING
IRONMONGER,
53 AND 55, YORKSHIRE STREET,
ROCHDALE.

IRON AND STEEL MERCHANT.

Kitchen Ranges, Register Grates, Marble Chimney Pieces, Chandeliers, Gas Tubes and Fittings, &c.

AGENT FOR ROCHDALE FOR THE

"HOME WASHER," MILNER'S SAFES,

CHEAVIN'S RAPID FILTERS, &c.

JOHN PETRIE, JUNR.,
MACHINIST AND IRON FOUNDER,
River Street Works,
ROCHDALE.

MAKER OF PATENT

PARAGON WOOL SCOURING
MACHINES,
REQUIRING NO LIFTING APPARATUS.

N.B.–New Improved Slide Lifter supplied to Old Machines.

IMPROVED HOT AIR WOOL DRYING.

The above are the most complete and serviceable Machines extant.

Archaeological excavation across the centre of the River Street site revealed the remains of a building, used initially as an iron foundry. The original footprint of the iron foundry measured 59m by 7.6m wide as demarcated by the four external walls, set on stone foundations. Other physical remains relating to the earliest phase of the foundry, which was constructed around 1819, comprised a vaulted basement annexe, a boiler bed with flue to a chimney, machine beds, a well, four brick tanks and exterior paved surfaces. The most common means of melting cast iron in the 19th century was in a cupola furnace and it is likely that this type of vertical, coke-fired furnace may have been utilised within the foundry. No evidence of a furnace was found during the excavation, but as the cupola was normally raised above the foundry floor, it is unlikely to have left any physical remains in the ground.

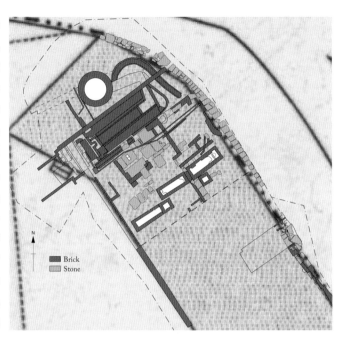

The base of a circular brick-built chimney was revealed adjacent to the northern wall of the building. The chimney served at least two flues that were connected to a boiler, which was represented by the well-preserved remains of a brick boiler base suitable in size to support a Cornish-type boiler. Other components of the boiler housing included an ash pit, the flame-end/rake-out area and a small basement used for storing coal.

Above right: Plan of early phase of iron foundry superimposed on the Ordnance Survey Town Plan, published in 1851

Right: Looking north-east across the boiler housing, with the annexe in the foreground (© Oxford Archaeology)

A cast-iron pipe probably used to supply water to the boiler crossed an internal space containing two large stone blocks with iron fixtures that likely represented machine beds. Four rectangular brick-built chambers set into the floor in the south of the building may have represented casting pits. In the south-eastern part of the building, there was evidence of power transmission in the form of several housings for bearing blocks.

The construction of new walls and the demolition of earlier ones indicated that the foundry had been significantly remodelled to create a larger floor area alongside the insertion of internal partitions and features. The modifications to the building included laying a new flagstone floor, blocking in the bearing boxes for lineshafts, removing the boiler in the northern part of the building and infilling its housing.

Top: Looking east at a possible lineshaft housing in a wall (© Oxford Archaeology)

Above: Bearing box housing in wall (© Oxford Archaeology)

Right: River Street brass foundry crucible pit (© Oxford Archaeology)

The works was occupied during the second half of the 19th century by John Petrie Junior, a manufacturer of textile machinery, including a wool-washing machine that he patented in 1853. The machine comprised an iron vessel or trough that contained soft soap and hot water, into which the wool was thrown and agitated by iron teeth. After being washed, the wool was drawn out of the vessel by a cylinder, set with iron teeth, and then subjected to a winnowing process that cleansed and dried the wool. Two fragments of wood, possibly derived from a carding machine or wool scourer designed by John Petrie Junior's company, were recovered during the excavation. Other finds from the site included 52 casting box mould core fragments formed from a mixture of compacted silica sand.

Left: Silica sand moulds and cores (© Oxford Archaeology)

Below: Wool scourer of a type that was patented by John Petrie in 1853

Bottom: Fragments derived from a wool scourer (© Oxford Archaeology)

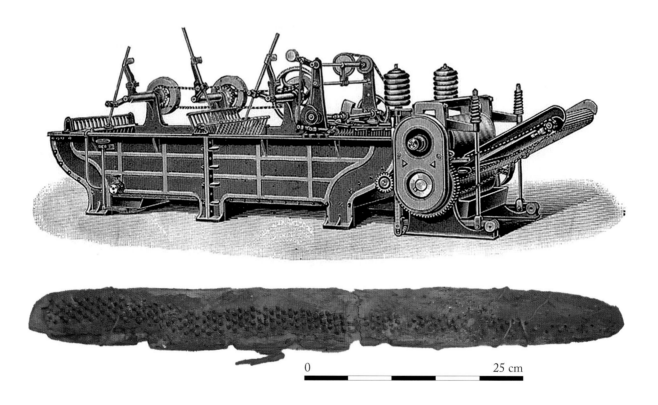

0   25 cm

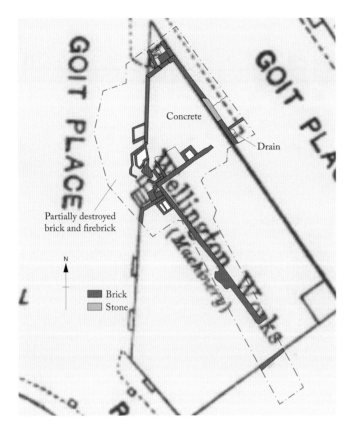

Above: Earlier remains of brass foundry superimposed on the Ordnance Survey Town Plan published in 1892

Below: The excavated remains of the extension to the brass foundry (© Oxford Archaeology)

The remains of a brass foundry, added to the works between 1831 and 1851, were discovered in the western part of the site. The walls of the earliest phase of the foundry were formed from two skins of hand-made bricks, suggesting that the foundry had been a single-storey structure, as the walls did not appear to be of sufficient strength to support the loading of additional floors. The original floor of the foundry had been laid with flagstones within which a series of holes had been made, likely to support fixtures such as a block and tackle used for lifting crucibles out of a crucible pit. A square structure measuring 0.92m x 0.92m and built of brick and stone was discovered adjacent to a network of flues within the foundry and probably represents the remains of a crucible pit.

As the brass foundry was too small to incorporate rolling facilities, which were used to make large brass objects, it seems likely that the foundry was intended to produce brass components for the machinery manufactured at the iron works.

The brass foundry had evidently been extended during the second half of the 19th century and continued to function into the early 20th century. This was reflected in renovations such as the laying of a concrete floor, the insertion of walls and *ad hoc* repairs.

Industrialisation caused a great increase in demand for leather goods. This was the case not only because of the extraordinary rise in population in industrial areas but also because leather components were used to connect together important parts of the machinery installed within the mills springing up across industrial towns. Thus, as industrialisation took hold in the late 18th and early 19th centuries, the growing market for leather goods supported the founding of many new tanneries in the expanding towns. This was the case in Rochdale and one such tannery, which came to be known as 'Roach Place Tannery', was revealed during archaeological excavations in 2010 and 2011, carried out by the Centre for Applied Archaeology at Kitchen Street.

Little is known about the early history of the tannery, although it may be shown on a map of 1831. No documentary sources from before the mid-19th century mention a tannery on the site and it is not clear who owned the structures depicted on the 1831 map or what their function was. However, an annotation on the Ordnance Survey map surveyed between 1844 and 1848 indicates that by then the site was certainly being used as a tannery. Meanwhile, census records from 1841 suggest that the smaller rectangular building in the east of the site was a dwelling known as 'Tan Pits', suggesting a link with tanning.

The earliest remains encountered during the archaeological works included part of the stone-built external wall of the tannery. Inside the eastern part of the building, a floor had been formed from a series of large flagstones, which were laid on either side of a drainage channel. This part of the tannery was interpreted as an area where fat and hair were scraped from the raw hides. Adjacent to this floor surface were the remains of at least five stone-lined tanks. The tanks were likely used to soak the de-fleshed hides in a solution of tannic acid, which loosened the hairs and allowed for the hides to be scoured.

A further set of tanks constructed using large sandstone slabs sealed with clay was revealed in the southern part of the building. These tanks may have been used for the tanning process that would ultimately transform the hide into leather. Tanning involved attaching the hides to a frame and immersing them for around three months in a weak solution of water or vegetable matter, known as tanning liquor or ooze. After this, the hides were then moved to pits with a more concentrated solution of tanning liquor and left there for an extended period.

Opposite

Top: *Kitchen Street site location (2010) superimposed on an extract from satellite imagery of 2005 (© Google)*

Bottom: *Kitchen Street site location superimposed on an extract from the Ordnance Survey six-inch plan of 1851*

This page

Top: *Remains of internal tanks, looking north-east. (© University of Salford)*

Middle: *Internal floor surface with central drainage channel (© University of Salford)*

Bottom: *Lime pits and rinsing tanks (source:* A Text-book of Tanning, *by Henry R. Procter, 1927)*

A network of stone-built culverts was exposed in the yard area to the east of the main building. The culverts contained deposits of vivid tan-coloured silt, which likely constituted residues associated with the tanning process.

The tannery continued to develop, with extensions added to the component buildings throughout the second half of the 19th century. An open-sided workshop, which appears to have been erected in the open yard to the immediate east of the earlier tannery building, may have been where 'currying' took place. Currying was the process in which the leather produced by the tanning process was made supple and involved soaking, scraping and treatment with tallow or 'train' oil. In the first half of the 19th century, the process of currying could not legally be carried out by tanners. However, a change in the law in 1851 allowed tanners to carry out this process. Trade directory entries and census information confirm that currying was being undertaken at the Roach Place Tannery during the second half of the 19th century.

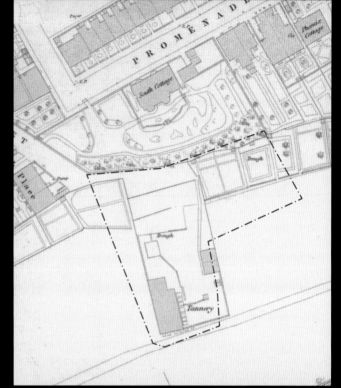

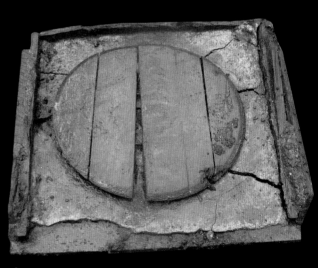

0   1 m

0   50 cm

east of the tannery appears to have been repurposed for an industrial function in the second half of the 19th century. Alongside the rebuilt and extended western wall of Tan Pits Place, a boiler room had been constructed. The boiler itself was discovered attached to an iron pipe that led through an aperture in the wall of Tan Pits Place.

During the early 1880s, the Cunliffe family went into partnership with the Jackson family, and the tannery became known as 'Roach Leather Works'. By 1894 Cunliffe and Jackson had relocated to alternative premises on River Street, but Roach Leather Works was still in use under the name of 'Ramsay Street Tanning and Currier Company'. No further entries for the tannery appear in the trade directories after 1894, and cartographic sources from the late 19th century show the site to be disused.

This page

Above: *Cast-iron boiler found close to its original setting within the boiler room (© University of Salford)*

Right: *Close-up view of the boiler house with the hexagonal boiler setting exposed. The cast-iron pipe leading into Tan Pits Place is also visible in the top right corner of the photograph (© University of Salford)*

Opposite

Above: *Kitchen Street site location superimposed on an extract from the Ordnance Survey Town Plan published in 1851*

Left: *Detail of a cork strip found during excavation (© University of Salford)*

Right: *Possible well cover with timber framing and plaster layer found during excavation (© University of Salford)*

0   50 cm

ROCHDALE RIVERSIDE PHASE I

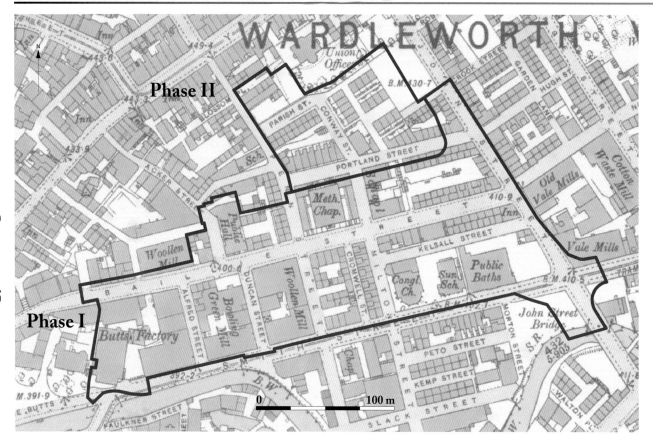

The Rochdale Riverside redevelopment focused around Baillie Street afforded a fantastic opportunity to investigate a large area in central Rochdale that had developed rapidly in the first half of the 19th century. The archaeological fieldwork began in 2018 with the excavation of eight evaluation trenches, the locations of which were recommended by GMAAS. The evaluation trenches were intended to confirm the survival of the remains of workers' housing and associated structures and features, such as communal privies and a Congregational church.

The results of the evaluation suggested that much of the site did not merit any further investigation because 20th-century development had removed all archaeological remains in many places. However, three areas in the eastern part of the site warranted further investigation. The excavation of these areas provided a fascinating insight into life in industrial Rochdale.

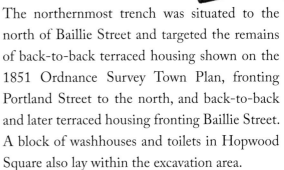

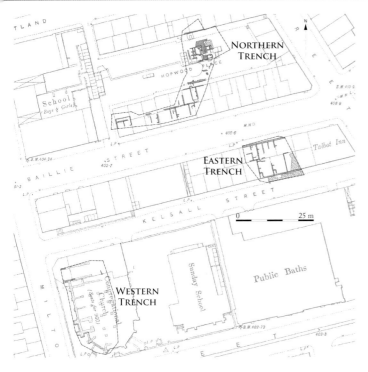

The northernmost trench was situated to the north of Baillie Street and targeted the remains of back-to-back terraced housing shown on the 1851 Ordnance Survey Town Plan, fronting Portland Street to the north, and back-to-back and later terraced housing fronting Baillie Street. A block of washhouses and toilets in Hopwood Square also lay within the excavation area.

The earliest deposit discovered in the northern trench was a soil horizon containing sherds of 17th- and 18th-century pottery and an 18th-century clay pipe bowl. This soil horizon was derived from the enclosed fields that occupied the site prior to the construction of workers' houses in the first half of the 19th century. The finds suggested that the fields were being night-soiled throughout the 17th and 18th centuries. Other features, including a portion of drystone walling and a circular feature thought to represent a pond, registered the agricultural or horticultural use of the site prior to urbanisation in the 19th century.

A wall composed of hand-made bricks was discovered at the northern edge of the trench, likely representing the southern front wall of a block of houses labelled on the 1851 Ordnance Survey Town Plan as Portland Place. The range of houses comprised two rows of what appear on the historic maps to be back-to-backs.

To the south of the houses was a cobbled courtyard, containing the remains of a small square building interpreted as washhouses or toilets serving Portland Place. The foundation of the southern wall of the washhouse was partially formed by a reused stone wall. This stone wall had probably been constructed in the 18th century when terraces were formed for the ornamental gardens associated with Town Head House, an impressive Georgian residence on Yorkshire Street. The walls of the washhouse comprised hand-made brick bonded with lime mortar, typical of the first half of the 19th century.

Outside privies serving multiple homes were common in the early to mid-19th century. However, this privy and washhouse are unusual in that they are depicted on the historical mapping until at least the 1950s and were probably demolished at the same time as the houses, during the 1960s.

Between the toilet block and Portland Place were the remains of a circular brick-built well that was capped with a large, thick stone slab. This well was marked on the 1851 Town Plan as 'pump'.

It was evident from the presence of walls utilising hard dark-grey mortar that the privy and washhouse had been enlarged between 1851 and 1891. This may be seen as a response to a series of national Acts that were introduced throughout the second half of the 19th century with the intention of improving housing conditions and sanitation.

The Local Government Act of 1858 gave towns the freedom to adopt clauses from the previous, unsuccessful, Towns Improvement Clauses Act of 1847 to enforce improvements to housing, such as the requirement for all houses to be built with drains. Alongside this Act was the Form of Bye-Laws of 1858 which fused elements of the 1855 Metropolitan Building Act with the Improvement Clauses Act into a set of regulations that could be enforced nationally. This Act required all houses to have a yard, the size of which was determined by the number of building storeys.

Although this Act was somewhat successful initially, increased housing needs due to the rapidly growing population caused these restrictions to be lifted in 1864. In 1868 The Torrens Act (part of the Artisans' and Labourers' Dwellings Act) provided for gradual improvement or demolition of sub-standard housing, but was largely ineffective. The Public Health Act of 1875, and the subsequent River Pollution Prevention Act of 1876, dealt with sanitation in housing, and led to the adoption of water closets and ash closets, from which the 'night soil' could be removed by 'night soil men' to designated disposal sites or to be used in a variety of industries. This system was particularly popular in Birmingham, Manchester and Rochdale, and it may be that the improvement to the privy block followed the introduction of this Act.

Opposite

Top: *Photograph showing the washhouse block (1), the toilet block (2) and later 19th-century extension wall (3), looking north-west*

Middle: *Photograph of the pump well in Portland Place*

Bottom: *The southern part of Portland Place courtyard, showing the remains of an earlier stone wall (centre)*

This page

Top: *The washhouse (1) and the toilet block (2) serving the houses along Portland Street and Baillie Street. The stone capping of the well can be seen in the foreground*

Middle: *A night soil collecting vehicle, Rochdale, c. 1870*

Right: *Fluted column discovered within demolition rubble in the northern part of the site*

0   1 m

In 1851 the 20 houses along Portland Street and the six on Baillie Street were served by at least four privies positioned in the yard that would come to be known as Hopwood Place. This amounted to one privy for every six or seven houses. In comparison, in Manchester at the same period the average was one privy per 12 houses. Similarly, in Manchester there was one pump for every 32 houses, whereas the pump uncovered during the excavation, and marked on the 1851 map, served 26 houses. As this was the case in 1851 it seems that the housing in Rochdale was built to a slightly higher standard of hygiene than that in neighbouring Manchester.

In the southern part of the trench were the remains of a row of back-to-back houses that had been constructed in two phases: the western part of the terrace before 1851, and the eastern after 1851 but before 1892. The western part of the trench exposed the remains of the southern three houses in a terrace consisting of a block of six back-to-back houses. When excavated, cellars were found beneath. Two of the cellars were partially excavated, revealing a partition wall running through the middle of each, creating two separate rooms. While the adjoining rooms were inaccessible from one another, an individual staircase led into each. It appeared that the western cellar room could be accessed from the house immediately above, whereas the eastern cellar room could only be accessed from the house that shared the northern party wall and fronted Hopwood Square.

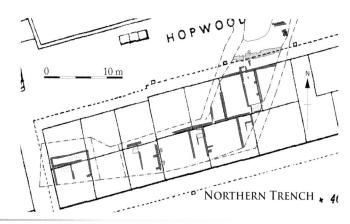

NORTHERN TRENCH

The eastern part of the terrace was formed by seven houses which historic maps suggest were built after 1851 and were slightly larger than the earlier houses at the western end of the terrace. Each house had its own cellar, probably functioning as a coal store – owing to the stone chutes housed in apertures in the external walls. These cellars extended across less than half the footprint of the house above. Access was provided by a curving stone-built staircase. Along one wall was a brick buttress, presumably supporting a fireplace in the room above. To the north of the terraced houses was a strip of cobbles that had probably formed a gutter running between the pavement and the surface of Hopwood Place, onto which the houses backed.

A trench excavated on the southern side of Kelsall Street targeted the footprint of Milton Street Congregational Church, a large stone Gothic Revival building seating a congregation of up to 900. The church was built with monetary support from the successful Rochdale flannel manufacturer Henry Kelsall. The church was demolished in the 1950s.

The excavation revealed the western side of the church's foundations, which in places survived to over 1m in height.

This page

Top: *The excavated remains of Milton Street Congregational Church, looking south (© University of Salford)*

Middle: *Milton Street Congregational Church before demolition in the 1950s (courtesy of Touchstones Rochdale)*

Bottom: *The remains recorded in the southern part of the northern trench superimposed over the 1891 Ordnance Survey Town Plan*

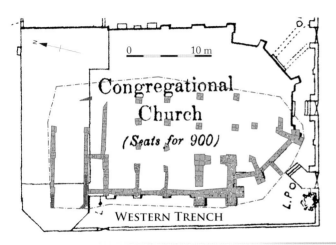

Opposite

Top: *Two of the excavated cellars (© University of Salford)*

Middle: *The remains of a cellar with the curving staircase, fireplace foundations and coal chute at the bottom right of the photograph (© University of Salford)*

Bottom: *The remains recorded in the southern part of the northern trench superimposed over the 1891 Ordnance Survey Town Plan (© University of Salford)*

Archaeologists discovered housing for a wooden staircase leading down into the church's crypt, which appeared to have had a vaulted ceiling. Beyond the northern wall of the church was an area that appeared to be a later addition, possibly for the installation of a boiler that had been connected to a heating system. In the central part of the church's footprint were the remains of column bases almost certainly used to support the floor and structure above.

A trench in the eastern part of the site exposed part of a block of back-to-backs with slightly larger houses fronting Baillie Street – the main thoroughfare, located to the north – and smaller properties fronting Kelsall Street to the south.

The excavation exposed the pavement of Kelsall Street and the foundations of four houses fronting onto it (numbered 1, 2, 3 and 4 on the photo), revealing that they were not cellared. Census returns for 1851 suggest that the houses on Kelsall Street were, at that time, occupied by skilled tradesmen associated with the local textile industry, including a machine maker and a foreman in a woollen mill. By the later 19th century the residents' occupations had become more homogenous and perhaps slightly lower status, being described exclusively as skilled mill operatives.

Top: The eastern trench superimposed onto the 1891 Ordnance Survey Town Plan (© University of Salford)

Middle: Photograph of the eastern trench fully excavated, looking east (© University of Salford)

Bottom: Rooms within the cellar of House 7. Note the remains of a probable 'cold slab' on the right of the photo (© University of Salford)

House 1 had a stone-flagged floor with a stone channel running into a ceramic drain along the inside of the house's front wall, an arrangement that was suggestive of an exterior space. The historic mapping suggests that between 1893 and 1910 the two easternmost houses along Kelsall Street had been incorporated into the Talbot Inn to their immediate east, which was located outside the excavation area.

The larger houses that fronted Baillie Street (numbered 5, 6 and 7 on the image opposite) were found to have had cellars split into smaller rooms furnished with coal chutes, fireplaces and stone-flagged floors. Interestingly, the visible brick walls in Houses 5 and 6 showed evidence of springing points for a brick-built barrel-vaulted ceiling, and the cellar in House 7 had multiple rooms, one of which contained a possible 'cold slab' (a stone slab used to keep cheese, milk and butter cool and usually located close to the floor).

Left: The pavement of Kelsall Street (left), front wall of House 1 (middle) and stone drain (right) (© University of Salford)

Right: Staircase, flagged floor, and fireplace foundations in House 6. Springing point for a barrel-vaulted ceiling visible at the left of the scale (© University of Salford)

It is notable that most of the houses recorded were either uncellared or only had small storage areas, whereas many houses of a similar date in Manchester or Salford had full-size cellars, which in many cases served as dwellings. This probably reflects a situation where there was less of a premium for space in Rochdale than in Manchester or Salford. The cellar layouts of the houses on Kelsall Street were not much altered, indicating that they had served their function adequately until they were demolished in the early 1970s.

Another indicator that working-class housing was of a relatively high standard in Rochdale is that large-scale 'slum' regeneration and improvement did not take place. In contrast, in Manchester, following a series of public health Acts, low-quality housing began to be cleared in the late 19th century. However, it could be that in Rochdale the Acts were simply ignored as low-quality housing was certainly present. For example, a building survey conducted in 1994 by the Royal Commission on the Historical Monuments of England at 13–16 Richard Street, near the canal basin, recorded a series of small back-to-back houses featuring cellar dwellings, which were probably built during the first two decades of the 19th century.

1871
ROCHDALE: 26
YORKSHIRE: 4
COLNE, LANCASHIRE: 2
BURY: 1
HEYWOOD: 1
LINCOLNSHIRE: 1
LONDON: 1
OLDHAM: 1

1881
ROCHDALE: 32
YORKSHIRE: 3
BOLTON: 1
BURNLEY: 1
LANCASHIRE: 1
MIDDLETON: 1
STAFFORDSHIRE: 1

1891
ROCHDALE: 32
DERBY: 3
LIVERPOOL: 2
GRIMSBY: 1
HEYWOOD: 1
SHROPSHIRE: 1

TYRONE PARISH
MAYO

1901
ROCHDALE: 21
NORFOLK: 3
CUMBRIA: 2
SHROPSHIRE: 2
ALDERSHOT, HAMPSHIRE: 1
HEYWOOD: 1
MIDDLETON: 1

1911
ROCHDALE: 26
MAYO, IRELAND: 3
BOLTON: 2
DUMBARTON, SCOTLAND: 1
TYRONE PARISH, DUNMORE, NORTHERN IRELAND: 1
OLDHAM: 1

This infographic presents census return data relating to the demographics of those inhabiting properties on Baillie and Kelsall streets between 1851 and 1911. Over the first few decades covered in the census, most of the residents had either been born locally or came from other parts of Yorkshire and Lancashire. From 1881 onwards a slightly higher proportion of the residents derived from other parts of England. It was not until 1911 that migrants from Ireland began to reside in the houses.

The data also reflects changes in the economy. Between 1851 and 1871 almost all the working occupants were employed in the wool industry. In 1881 most of the residents are described as being employed in either wool or cotton product manufacturing. However, from 1891 onwards a more diverse list of trades is recorded and a policeman and an electrical engineer were two notable residents of Baillie Street in 1881 and 1901 respectively.

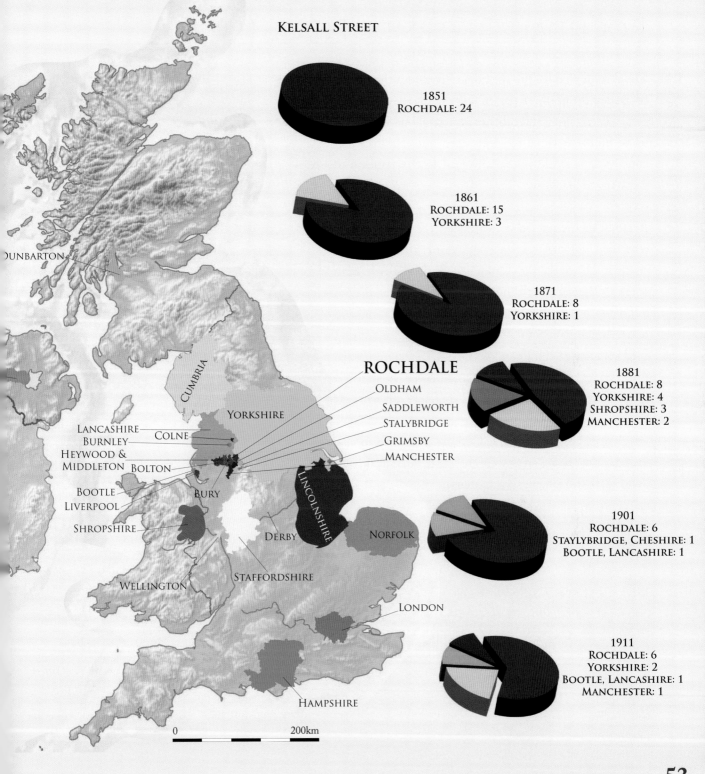

KELSALL STREET

1851
ROCHDALE: 24

1861
ROCHDALE: 15
YORKSHIRE: 3

1871
ROCHDALE: 8
YORKSHIRE: 1

1881
ROCHDALE: 8
YORKSHIRE: 4
SHROPSHIRE: 3
MANCHESTER: 2

1901
ROCHDALE: 6
STAYLYBRIDGE, CHESHIRE: 1
BOOTLE, LANCASHIRE: 1

1911
ROCHDALE: 6
YORKSHIRE: 2
BOOTLE, LANCASHIRE: 1
MANCHESTER: 1

DUNBARTON

CUMBRIA

YORKSHIRE

ROCHDALE

OLDHAM
SADDLEWORTH
STALYBRIDGE
GRIMSBY
MANCHESTER

LANCASHIRE
BURNLEY
HEYWOOD &
MIDDLETON
COLNE
BOLTON

BOOTLE
LIVERPOOL
BURY

SHROPSHIRE

LINCOLNSHIRE

DERBY
NORFOLK

STAFFORDSHIRE

WELLINGTON

LONDON

HAMPSHIRE

0   200km

ROCHDALE RIVERSIDE PHASE II

The second phase of the Rochdale Riverside scheme was centred in the northern part of the overall redevelopment area, where a hotel and other commercial buildings were to be built. As these required deep foundations, their construction would potentially lead to the removal of surviving archaeology.

A study of historic maps suggested that the site had remained largely undeveloped until the mid-19th century. However, the Ordnance Survey Town Plan of 1891 showed that the entire site was covered with buildings by this time, reflecting the population and house-building boom that Rochdale experienced during the 1860s and 1870s. Therefore, GMAAS recommended that a trial trench evaluation be undertaken. In addition to revealing the well-preserved remains of workers' houses, the fragmentary remains of Nazareth Chapel, which had been built along Conway Street, were also found. Three larger areas were then excavated to further investigate the remains encountered.

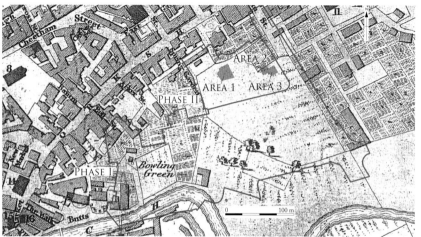

Left: The boundary of the Phase 2 redevelopment area superimposed onto Murphy's map of 1831 (© University of Salford)

Above: Locations of archaeological excavation areas superimposed on Google satellite imagery from 2017 (© University of Salford)

Right: The remains of possible commercial property at Crook Street looking south-east. The exterior wall fronting Crook Street is in the foreground. A partition wall and the partially surviving flagstone floor of the property's cellar are visible to the left of the scale. The small rectangular chambers to the right are later additions (© University of Salford)

Far right: Fragmentary remains of two houses on the upper terrace fronting Parish Street, looking north-east (© University of Salford)

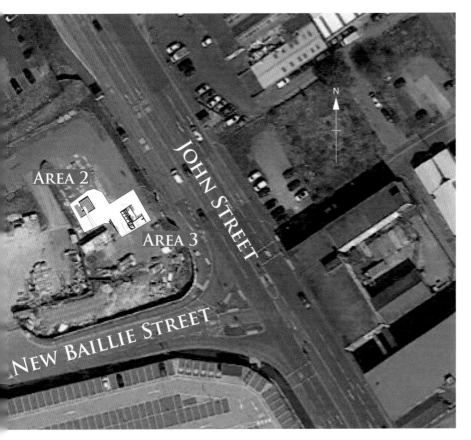

The earliest remains recorded on the site were in Area 3, where the remains of properties on Crook Street and Portland Yard, constructed in the early 19th century, were revealed. The excavation area fell over the footprint of an irregular-shaped building attached to the south-west end of a row of back-to-back houses. Murphy's map indicates that Crook Street had not been constructed by 1831, but census returns document residents living there in 1841 – the year of the first census. This suggests that the properties must have been built between 1831 and 1841.

The northern and western walls of the irregular-shaped building – which was probably a pair of back-to-back houses – were revealed in the trench. The remains of a partition dividing two rooms within the building, along with the remains of a flagstone-paved floor, were exposed. The second of these rooms, to the south-west of the partition, contained a brick-built fireplace with an upright flagstone used to line the back of the fireplace and a sandstone hearth on the floor. Immediately to the west of the building was a large covered entrance providing access from Crook Street to Portland Yard.

During the 1850s the large plot of open ground depicted on the 1851 Ordnance Survey Town Plan to the west of Crook Street was built over with rows of terraced houses, many of which were back-to-backs. Area 1 was positioned to investigate the eastern end of a row of back-to-back dwellings and sanitary blocks at the corner of Parish Street and Conway Street that had been built on the open ground. It is known that the houses were constructed after 1851 but before 1861 when the census returns register the dwellings.

Centre: Excavation areas superimposed on the 1891 Ordnance Survey Town Plan (© University of Salford)

Opposite: A photograph taken in 1970 looking north up Penn Street, showing the south-west end of Maude Terrace: the back-to-back houses in the centre of the photograph (courtesy of Touchstones Rochdale)

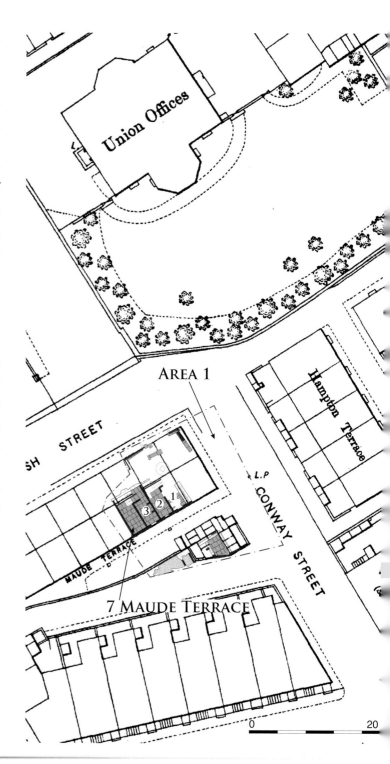

AREA 2

AREA 3

CROOK STREET

M.H.

Argyle Terrace

Harcourt Terrace

...errace

PORTLAND Y

IRREGULAR-SHAPED
BUILDING

COVERED ENTRANCE

STREET

...TLAND

439·5 L.P·

N

The excavation revealed that the site's natural topography sloped steeply up towards the north and that the block of back-to-backs was built over two steps, or terraces, cut into the hillside. The houses fronting Parish Street were built on the upper step, those known as Maude Terrace on the lower step. A substantial stone wall about half a metre thick was built against the face of the earth terrace as a retaining wall to prevent the collapse of the step. The flagstone foundations of the houses fronting Parish Street were laid on natural clay and it was clear that no cellars were present beneath these properties.

The remains of two dwellings fronting Maude Terrace were exposed to the south, backing onto the houses fronting Parish Street. As with Parish Street, the brick walls forming the houses were built on flagstone foundations. However, cellars were present beneath these structures, and their layout was similar to those discovered beneath the excavated row of back-to-backs fronting Baillie Street.

At Maude Terrace – as at Baillie Street – the cellar occupying the footprint of each house was divided by a partition into two equally sized rectangular rooms. Beneath both dwellings, the south-western cellar was accessed from within the house immediately above while the north-eastern cellar room was accessed via stairs leading from the house behind, which fronted Parish Street. This arrangement likely reflected a response to the steeply sloping topography of the land on which the houses were built. Considerably less earth would need to be removed to create a cellar beneath the row of houses on the lower part of a slope than beneath the properties higher up the slope.

The cellars had flagstone floors, and two of them had recesses built into the upper courses of their front external walls. These recesses probably represented the remains of a small window light or coal chute. In many cases, features such as these were not depicted on historic maps, exemplifying how useful archaeological investigation is for recording and understanding the details of historic structures.

In the eastern cellar, the partition that separated the two rooms showed evidence of alteration, with a small section being knocked through to create a doorway between the two rooms. It is likely, although this could not be proven, that the entire cellar became accessible to one property rather than continuing to be a space which was split between two. This alteration was probably made in the early 20th century.

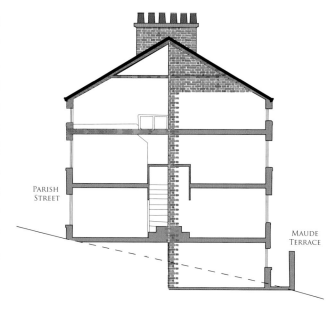

PARISH STREET

MAUDE TERRACE

Above: Representative sectional drawing through row of back-to-backs (© University of Salford)

Below: Knocked-through doorway between Rooms 1 and 2, and staircase for Room 1, looking south-east (© University of Salford)

Amongst the artefacts recovered from the backfill of the demolished buildings were stoneware jam jars, which are a common find in later 19th- and early 20th-century excavations. The example depicted was recovered from the cellar below No. 6 Maude Terrace. Such jars were very often reused for storage or even used as paint pots.

The producer of the jam jar, William Hartley, started off small, running a grocer's shop in Pendle, Lancashire. The story told is that in 1871 a supplier failed to deliver a consignment of jam, so William made his own. Such was the growth of the company that by 1898 W. P. Hartley, then based in Liverpool, took over a pottery in Rutherglen, near Glasgow, thereby ensuring its own supply of jam jars. As in the example depicted, the maker's mark is impressed on the base, with the proviso that the jar is "NOT GENUINE UNLESS BEARING WᵐP. HARTLEY'S LABEL." Colourful paper labels likely adorned the jar when new. The pottery closed in 1929, and by the early 1930s Hartley's jam was being sold in glass jars.

Above: The cellar below No. 7 Maude Terrace (© University of Salford)

Right: Hartley's stoneware jar from Maude Terrace (© University of Salford)

Below: Stairs serving the cellar below No. 6 (© University of Salford)

0　　　　　　　　　10 cm

An object found during the excavation that connects the homes of those who lived in early to mid-20th-century Maude Terrace to most of us today is the fridge, two almost identical examples of which were discovered in the cellars below Nos. 6 and 7. These early fridges consisted of a large white-glazed ceramic 'box' with internal ribs which would have supported metal shelves. The maker's mark reveals that 'THE "FRIDGE" LARDER' was 'made only by J. Duckett & Son Ltd, Burnley.' The rather curious construction material – ceramic rather than enamel, metal and plastic – can probably be explained by the 1913 catalogue published by J. Duckett & Son. The company specialised in sanitary wares such as ceramic water closets, urinals and basins, some with aspirational names such as the 'Kensington' or the 'Victoria,' while others named in an advert from 1898 were less appealing, such as 'The Clencher'.

Amongst the other artefacts recovered from the backfill of the demolished houses were two almost complete large storage vessels, which were reconstructed after the excavation had finished. These large jars, usually described as cream pots for the smaller vessel and bread pots for the larger, were found in the cellar below No. 6 Maude Terrace. The shape of these jars are typical of East Lancashire and West Yorkshire. No potteries of this type are known in Rochdale, although the Grimshaw pottery near Blackburn was still in operation in c. 1846. At Halifax, some 22km to the north-east of Rochdale, there were potteries in existence on the steep eastern side of the town from the 1640s until the 1880s. At Soil Hill, also near Halifax, Isaac Button was still producing large pancheons (ceramic bowls) and stew pots into the early 1960s.

0   10 cm

Opposite: The two fridge larders discovered in the cellars of Nos. 6 and 7 Maude Terrace during excavation (© University of Salford)

Above: Cream pot from the cellar below No. 6 Maude Terrace (© University of Salford)

Right: A two-handled brown-glazed storage vessel reconstructed after the excavation (© University of Salford)

THE "FRIDGE" LARDER

REGᴰ TRADE MARK

No ⸱ᵞ⸱ ᵌ90. ⁄

WATSON'S PATENT

No 3Ɑ50'ᵌ

MADE ONLY F ⸱➤

J. DUCKETT & SON Lᵀᴰ

BURNLEY.

Despite the commercialisation and industrialisation of food and drink that can be discerned in the finds from houses in Rochdale, there is evidence of more local, small-scale production of goods continuing in the towns of Lancashire and Yorkshire by so-called 'country potters'. Although factories producing transfer-printed tablewares had been a feature of the North Midlands and Northern England since the late 18th century, coarse wares, vessels for food preparation and storage or for use in dairies, were still the preserve of the country potter – often family-run businesses with one or two kilns.

Development in Rochdale town centre dating to the 1870s was recorded in Area 2, where the remains of two double-depth terrace dwellings along Argyle Terrace, first depicted cartographically in 1891, were recorded. The census returns, which were compiled every ten years, first recorded residents living in the dwellings in 1881 but not in 1871.

0   20 cm

The vestiges of the structure exposed in the north-east part of the excavation area corresponded to the end-of-terrace property known as No. 8 Argyle Terrace. The cellar had a flagged floor that had been truncated in the north-east corner, revealing a narrow stone-capped drain with brick-built sides. A single-skin wall formed a partition between the cellar in No. 8 and the cellar in No. 6. This wall had presumably been disturbed by a modern service pipe that ran parallel to it. The modern service may have also truncated or concealed a staircase that would have permitted access into the cellar.

The partial remains of No. 6 Argyle Terrace consisted of a flagged floor and two buttresses protruding from the partition wall that presumably supported a fireplace in the room above.

The cellars beneath Argyle Terrace did not occupy the entire footprint of the house and so it was suggested by the excavator that they represented cold stores. A similar arrangement was observed during an archaeological excavation at Toad Lane in the Lower Falinge area of Rochdale, and it thus appears that the local vernacular for domestic buildings included half-cellars.

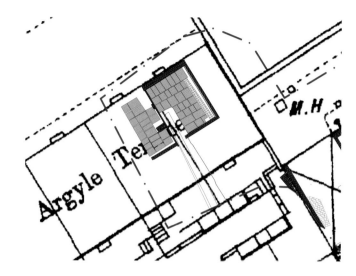

Top: *Plan of Area 2 superimposed onto the Ordnance Survey Town Plan of 1891 (© University of Salford)*

Middle: *Area 2, looking south-east (© University of Salford)*

Bottom: *Area 1, with fireplace, looking north-west (© University of Salford)*

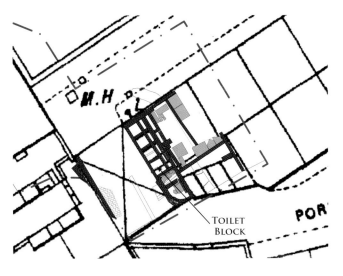

TOILET BLOCK

POR

Archaeological features pertaining to the late 19th century were represented by two sanitary-related structures recorded in Area 3. The fact that the late 19th-century archaeology was represented by sanitary-related structures almost certainly reflects the measures brought in from the mid-19th century – described on page 47 – that sought to improve the living conditions afforded by working-class housing.

In the southern part of the trench, a structure likely representing a block of privies or wash facilities was found abutting No. 4 Portland Yard and No. 4 Crook Street. The remains of the structure consisted of four small rectangular chambers with a stone-capped culvert running beneath.

In the centre of the trench were the remains of another sanitary-related structure. This building also contained four small chambers with a drainage system running between them. The presence of drains and the size and shape of the compartments imply that the structures functioned as privies. However, it seems that the addition of the toilet block caused damp-related problems for No. 4 Crook Street where, it was observed, an extra skin of bricks had been added internally, probably to mitigate against seepage from the toilet block.

Top: A plan of the remains recorded in Area 3 superimposed onto the Ordnance Survey Town Plan of 1891 (© University of Salford)

Bottom: Stone setts bordered by a wall, and the channel in the centre and toilet block structure to the east, looking north (© University of Salford)

TOAD LANE

The area surrounding Toad Lane, to the north-west of Rochdale town centre, could be characterised as a semi-rural part of Rochdale until the late 19th century. Prior to this open fields covered much of the area, with ribbon development in the form of blocks of back-to-back houses and other terraced dwellings strung along Toad Lane and Falinge Road.

The footprint of some of these semi-rural houses was investigated by Salford Archaeology in 2017 as part of redevelopment works to renew social housing built in the 1960s. A single archaeological trench was opened off Toad Lane in the Lower Falinge Estate, which sought to investigate the remains of an early 19th-century block of four workers' houses shown on the 1851 Ordnance Survey Town Plan of the area.

Two parallel walls identified across the excavation area represented the foundations of the front and rear elevations of the four cottages, which had clearly been built as a single block. A third wall that was revealed along the centre of the cottages, parallel to the external walls, evidently represented a partition that created front and rear rooms in each cottage. All of the walls were constructed from mixed courses of hand-made bricks and sandstone blocks bonded with two different types of mortar.

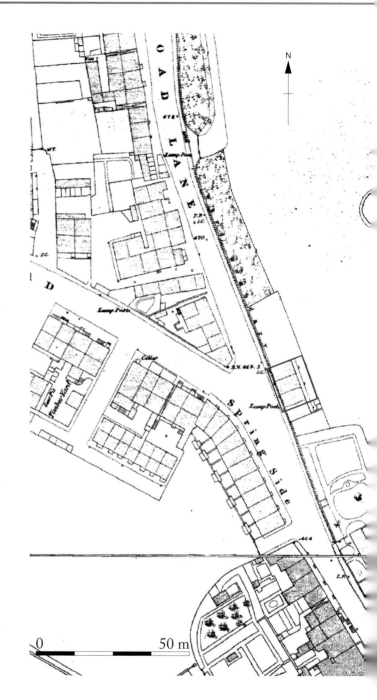

Excavation demonstrated that each of the cottages had a cellar beneath the rear room. The cellars were divided by several single-course internal partitions that abutted the main external walls and were constructed of hand-made bricks. One unusual feature of the houses at Toad Lane, however, was that the cellar dividing walls appeared to have been inserted rather than keyed into the main rear and central walls. This implies that the main structure of the block was constructed as a shell which was then divided into individual houses. This is a slightly unusual building technique, which suggests that the houses were possibly built by a small-scale landowner rather than an experienced property speculator.

Opposite

Excavation boundary superimposed on Ordnance Survey Town Plan of 1851 (© University of Salford)

This page

Above: *Overview of the trench. Main external walls of the terrace house can be seen amongst the demolition rubble (© University of Salford)*

Below: *Excavated cellar and staircase. Black coal dust is visible on the whitewashed walls (© University of Salford)*

One key indicator that helped the archaeologists recognise that these were cellars was the presence of several sets of curving stone steps. These steps were built of dressed stone flags with some structural elements constructed of hand-made bricks. Both stone staircases were partly enclosed by a brick-built stairwell. The positioning of the steps suggested to the archaeologists that these cellars were accessed from inside the houses.

Each cellar had a flagstone floor with some black staining thought to be coal dust. The cellar walls also showed evidence of being painted or whitewashed, with the black staining also identified on the whitewash. This black staining suggested that the cellars were used to store coal – needed to fuel domestic fires for heating and cooking. None of the cellars contained any internal features such as light fittings and fireplaces, reflecting their intended use for just cold storage.

Excavation revealed that very little of the front rooms to the cottages survived, with the internal floors having been removed completely during demolition. The only features that remained were small square structures built from a single course of hand-made bricks and bonded with lime-base mortar, consistent with an early 19th-century construction date. These structures represented the ash pits beneath the fireplaces in each of the front rooms.

To the west of the external wall fronting Toad Lane were the fragmentary remains of a stone-flagged surface and an area of cobbled stones. These features were thought to be external surfaces around doorways and small paved areas at the front of the houses between the front doors and the original pavement of Toad Lane.

Above: Remains of front room with fireplace. The black areas are burnt coal and cinder deposits (© University of Salford)

Below: Close-up of brick fireplace (© University of Salford)

When the houses were built in the early 19th century, they were located on the north-western fringe of the town within an area still dominated by agriculture. At this time the main built-up areas included buildings fronting onto the main thoroughfares of Toad Lane and Falinge Road with agricultural land behind. These dwellings represented the further expansion of workers' housing into the agricultural surroundings of Rochdale. The housing on Toad Lane was built on land formerly used as an orchard within the grounds of a large manor house, Quarry Hill, to the north of the site, and it is possible they were built to house employees of the Quarry Hill estate. This was owned during the early 19th century by Jonathan Fildes Esq., although it is unclear whether the houses were built by him.

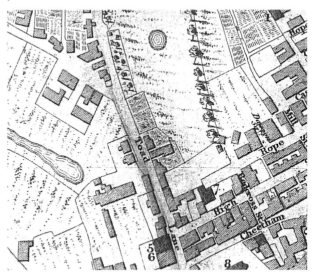

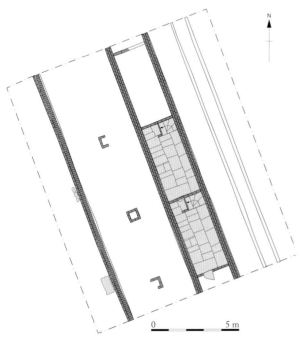

Top left: Close-up of cellar steps constructed of flagstones and brick (© University of Salford)

Above: Toad Lane on Murphy's map of 1831

Left: Archaeological trench plan – showing walls and cellar floors (© University of Salford)

ROCHDALE BRIDGE

In the heart of Rochdale, part of the River Roch was completely covered over by a series of bridges that had been built incrementally across the river. The original medieval bridge was widened in 1821 to improve the roadway, making it easier for traffic to move across the river, and to repair parts of the bridge that had become dangerous. In 1857, a prominent visitor to Rochdale described the town as having 'a little bridge that spans like a rocking horse an imaginary stream in which there is nothing liquid but mud…the town is in the shape of a tea-cup, with a gutter at the bottom.'

This appears to have been the prevailing opinion of the Roch and by the early 20th century it had been decided that the river should be covered, starting with the section between Yorkshire Street and Wellington Bridge, to build a tramway interchange. By 1924 most of the river in the centre of Rochdale had been enclosed, much of it using Hennebique's patented reinforced-concrete construction system – an early and important example of this ground-breaking new technology.

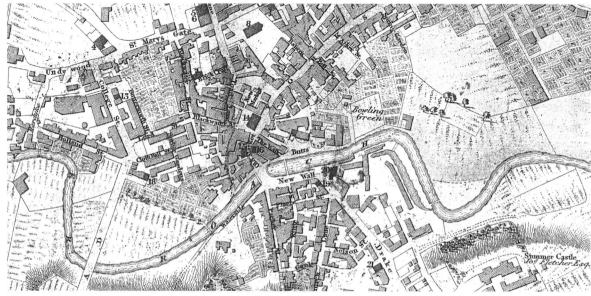

In 2011 work was begun to once again 'daylight' the river by removing parts of the extended bridge which had been added since the 17th century. The scheme to open the river was intended to reduce flood risk in the town centre, attract new wildlife into the area, and provide a view of the historic original bridge. Oxford Archaeology North was commissioned to investigate and record various spans of the 20th-century bridge that were to be removed.

Rochdale Bridge was an important part of the town's infrastructure, connecting the historic core on the south side of the river with the focus of Georgian expansion on the northern bank. The bridge was essential for hauliers conveying goods along the trans-Pennine route on which the local woollen economy relied.

It is not known when the first bridge across the Roch was constructed, although it seems likely that it existed by 1324 when a document refers to 'John of the Brig'. The river was also crossed via a ford in the vicinity of The Butts, which was referred to in early 17th-century documents. The ford remained in active use until the late 19th century, by which date local journalist and historian William Robertson stated that it 'was often made so deep by heavy rainfall as to become both inconvenient and dangerous.'

Centre: *A view from beneath Rochdale Bridge before removal of 20th-century bridge spans (© Oxford Archaeology)*

Above: *The ford across the River Roch at The Butts, c. 1810 (courtesy of Touchstones Rochdale)*

Left: *Wood's Plan of Rochdale, 1831*

Historic documents state that in 1676 the bridge needed repair work, suggesting that by this time it may have been of considerable antiquity. The bulk of the cost for the repair work was expended on transporting large quantities of stone.

The battlement of the historic bridge partially collapsed in November 1820 when a large crowd pressed upon it for a view of a bull bait that took place on the bed of the river. This incident caused the death of 11 people and led to a new bridge being added to the western side of the original Rochdale Bridge in 1821. The new bridge was 13 feet wide (3.96m) and was constructed in a Gothic Revival style with pointed arches. It improved the ease of movement of carts and stagecoaches across the river, whilst the original bridge was used mainly by pedestrians.

Soon after the construction of the 1821 bridge, a 7-foot wide (2.13m) extension was added to its eastern side, with a change in style from pointed to circular arches. This extension was likely made to allow carriages to pass in either direction on the deck of the bridge, evidencing the growth of commerce and trade in the town during the 19th century as the textile industry boomed. A 10-foot wide (3m) extension was also added to the western side of the bridge which featured cutwaters, each with simple, decorative buttresses and dentillated voussoirs (a wedge-shaped stone used in building an arch or vault).

Centre: *Artist's impression of c. 1820, showing the bull bait, Rochdale Bridge and the ford (courtesy of Touchstones Rochdale)*

Right: *The feeder bridge to the west of the 1821 bridge (courtesy of Touchstones Rochdale)*

A decision was reached in 1864 to widen the bridge by another 12 feet (3.66m), together with the construction of a massive stone river wall. Two polished granite commemorative stones, each bearing the Corporation arms, were placed in the parapet walls of the new bridge, which opened to traffic in 1869.

Following the linking together of the old Rochdale Bridge and the 1821 bridge in the 1860s, the retaining wall on either side of the river channel was rebuilt along with a flat-decked, curved feeder bridge, to the west of the 1821 bridge. Interestingly, the supports facing the cutwaters of the feeder bridge were designed by Sir Horace Jones, the London City Architect, in 1884, and are identical to those of Tower Bridge in London.

In 1881, Rochdale was granted an order under an amendment of the 1870 Tramways Act to construct a tramway in the town. The Wellington Bridge was duly built at the bottom of Drake Street in 1882 for the sole purpose of carrying the tramway over the river, on an angled alignment. It was constructed of typical railway engineering materials, with the heavy use of riveted wrought-iron girders, brick jack-arches, and sandstone abutments. The flat deck that was required by the tramway was carried on eight substantial I-section wrought-iron beams of riveted plate construction. At the time of the archaeological survey, the beams were supported by rectangular-section concrete columns, although these probably encased earlier cast-iron cylindrical columns that will have been typically used in the 1880s.

Above: Walk Bridge with Wellington Bridge in background, before river covering c. 1900 (courtesy of Touchstones Rochdale)

Additions to Rochdale Bridge in the early 20th century essentially led to the culverting of the river beneath the town. New technology and engineering practices utilising reinforced concrete were introduced at the start of the 20th century. All the reinforced concrete beam and slab sections used to construct new parts of the bridge were designed by LG Mouchel and Partners and cast on site using the Hennebique system.

The first section of the reinforced concrete bridge was built in 1904, filling the gap between the Rochdale and Wellington bridges. It was one of the earliest examples of the use of reinforced concrete in girder bridge construction in Britain. The Esplanade Bridge was built shortly after to create a 50m-wide extension on the western side of Rochdale Bridge, forming a road junction with Newgate.

Further extensions of the bridge covering the River Roch were undertaken between 1923 and 1924. Town Meadows Bridge was built in 1923, to the west of Esplanade Bridge, whilst Bus Station Bridge was built in 1924 to the east of Wellington Bridge.

In 1996 the Esplanade Bridge and Rochdale Bridge widening was deemed unsafe. Parts were subsequently demolished and replaced with new bridge sections supported by rolled steel joists.

Top: *Building the reinforced concrete bridge between Rochdale and Wellington bridges, 1904 (courtesy of Touchstones Rochdale)*

Bottom: *Testing the 1904 reinforced concrete rbridge, c. 1904 (courtesy of Touchstones Rochdale)*

Above: *Beneath the 1904 reinforced concrete bridge (courtesy of Touchstones Rochdale)*

Left: *Smith Street covering, 1924 (courtesy of Touchstones Rochdale)*

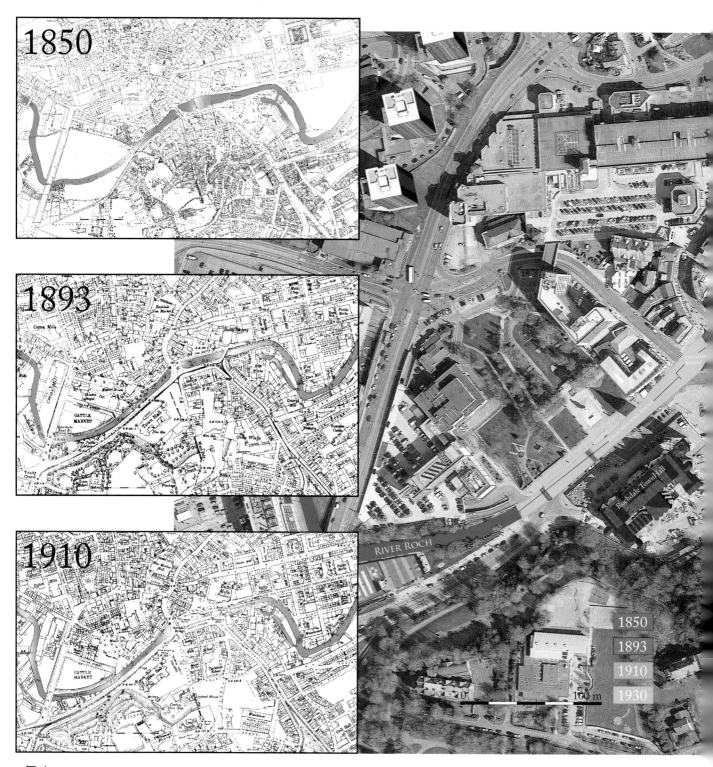

1850

1893

1910

RIVER ROCH

1850
1893
1910
1930

Rochdale Town Hall

0   100 m

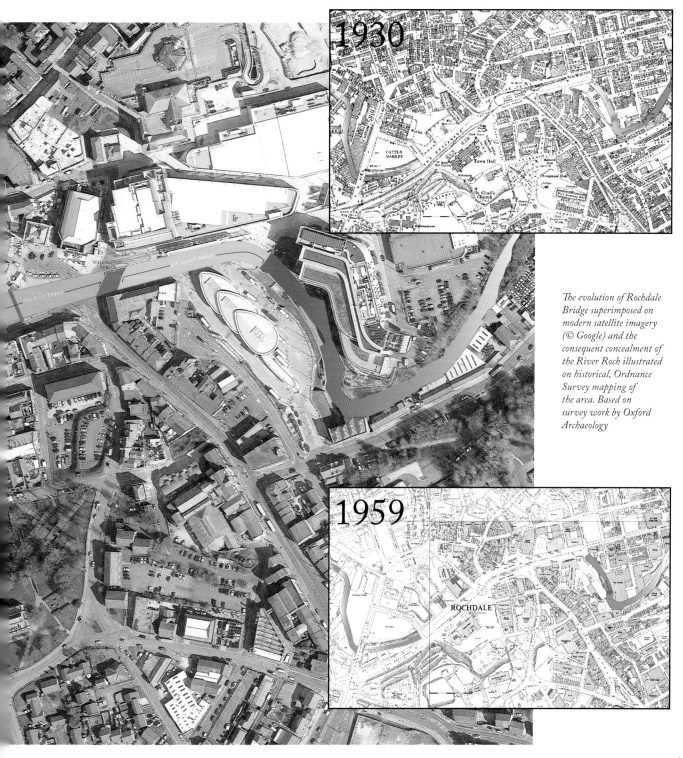

1930

1959

*The evolution of Rochdale
Bridge superimposed on
modern satellite imagery
(© Google) and the
consequent concealment of
the River Roch illustrated
on historical, Ordnance
Survey mapping of
the area. Based on
survey work by Oxford
Archaeology*

ROCHDALE TOWN HALL SQUARE

In 2021, the Rochdale Development Agency commenced work on a multi-million-pound restoration of Rochdale Town Hall, funded by Rochdale Council and the National Lottery Heritage Fund. The associated development of new public realm in Town Hall Square, and the regeneration of the Broadfield Park Slopes to the rear of the building, provided opportunities to investigate an area around Packer Street that is likely to have been at the core of the medieval and post-medieval town.

Packer Street links the ancient parish church to the medieval bridge over the river and probably derives its name from its use as a packhorse route. It was described in 1600 as 'the leading business street' in Rochdale and is shown on plans dating to 1757 and 1764 to have been lined with buildings, which included merchants' houses, warehouses, stabling and inns to serve the packhorse trade. Land to the rear of the properties along the west side of Packer Street included a large formal garden associated with a villa residence known as 'The Wood', together with the Roch Foundry, which had been established by the 1790s as one of the earliest iron and brass foundries in the town.

Most of the buildings lining the western side of Packer Street had been cleared by 1866 to enable the construction of Town Hall Square, which enclosed Rochdale Town Hall, the magnificent Gothic Revival edifice housing the civil servants of the newly created Municipal Borough of Rochdale.

The excavation of a series of test pits revealed the remains of structures and layers of relict soil concentrated in the south-eastern part of Town Hall Square. It was concluded that the site, and especially the area around the southern end of Packer Street, had potential for further archaeological investigation.

Above: Image of the town hall by Edward Walker, 1875

Below: Photograph of the southern end of Packer Street with Church Steps behind (courtesy of Touchstones Rochdale)

Opposite: The Rochdale Town Hall community excavation, in blue, and further investigation in the form of excavated trenches and test pits, in green, on the slopes to the south of Rochdale Town Hall. These are superimposed on the 1844 Castleton tithe map that shows Packer Street, which ran from St Chad's Church to the bridge, and also shows the density of buildings and the iron foundry

Discussion between GMAAS, the Rochdale Development Agency and the National Lottery Heritage Fund concluded that there was considerable scope for a community-led excavation where local people could actively explore Rochdale's archaeology. Therefore, in the summer of 2021 a large trench was excavated by community participants, and also school and youth groups, who were provided with training, guidance and support by staff from Salford Archaeology. Volunteer participation involved a range of activities including excavation and finds processing, and participants were also encouraged to take part in the archaeological recording of the site. Building on the success of the project, another community-led excavation was implemented in 2023, which targeted the footprint of historic buildings that had occupied the Broadfield Park Slopes together with any areas that offered potential for post-medieval or even medieval remains.

The archaeological excavation in 2021 comprised a single trench that measured 50m long by 8m wide in the southern part, reducing to 4m wide in the northern part. The excavation targeted the rear yards of properties fronting Packer Street, which were demolished during the construction of Town Hall Square in the 1860s.

The earliest deposit uncovered in the excavation was a cultivation layer from which sherds of late 17th-century and mid-18th-century pottery were recovered

A substantial brick wall was discovered in the southern part of the trench. This wall, which appeared to have been constructed in the mid-18th century, was orientated north-east by south-west and was constructed of hand-made bricks with a stone foundation. The wall likely formed a boundary between properties fronting Packer Street to the east and the gardens of The Wood to the west. A layer of silty garden soil was identified on the western side of the wall, likely representing horticultural activity within the grounds of The Wood. On the eastern side of the boundary wall, a long rectangular brick building with a well-made stone slab floor surface was revealed. This building, which had been built before 1844 when it is depicted on the tithe map, extended from the back of properties fronting Packer Street and could have been used as a workshop. It is known from documentary evidence that small-scale 'cottage' production was active along Packer Street during the 19th century. At 13 Packer Street for instance, Mary Casson, the wife of a woollen weaver, and her son Samuel supplemented the family's earnings by making ginger beer. The whole family showed an entrepreneurial spirit with Mary's daughter Elizabeth making toffee and another confectionery, whilst the youngest, Alice, was a dressmaker. By 1871 the business – now run by Samuel Casson – had grown and moved to larger premises on Molesworth Street. Here they manufactured mineral water and sold a wide variety of alcoholic and non-alcoholic beverages.

0   5 cm

The workshop had been demolished and replaced by a small toilet block by the mid-19th century. This housed two individual latrines that had been filled with ash and 'dry waste' including fragments of pottery, which was often used to seal latrines when they were put out of use later in the 19th century.

In the southern part of the trench another, larger, toilet block was recorded. This had two entrances, an internal brick-lined pit, and a floor consisting of a stone slab inscribed with the letter 'W' or 'M'. To the east and north of the buildings described above were roughly made external surfaces constructed from an assortment of different reused materials, and also a brick drain capped with reused stone roof tiles.

These structures were demolished during the late 19th century, and the area was levelled. The demolition material was then covered with a new yard surface, formed of glazed bricks which had probably been specially chosen for their hard-wearing qualities. When superimposed on the Ordnance Survey Town Plan of 1891 it could be seen that the southern part of the trench, where the glazed-brick surface was recorded, falls within an open area that was accessed from Packer Street via a covered entrance beneath a building fronting the street.

Opposite

Top: *Looking east of late 18th-/early 19th-century boundary wall with later structures behind (© University of Salford)*

Bottom: *Ginger beer bottle from the period when Samuel Casson was running the company, around 1871. Recovered during the excavation at Rochdale Town Hall, summer 2021 (© University of Salford)*

This page

Top: *19th-century yard surface looking north-west (© University of Salford)*

Bottom: *Inscribed stone slab in floor of outbuilding (© University of Salford)*

An intriguing spread of stone chippings and roughly worked sandstone blocks was found in the western part of the excavation area. This may have indicated the position where masons chiselled out ashlar blocks before they incorporated them into the walls of the town hall. Above this, the entire northern and central parts of the excavation area were sealed with made ground formed from tips of sand, industrial waste such as clinker and ash, and demolition material up to 2m thick. This had been used to level off the slope down to the river and create a level bedding on which to construct Town Hall Square. This was presumably established by 1871 when the town hall was completed. It could be seen in the section of the trench that the 19th-century layers were covered by thinner layers of made ground and tarmac that represented the resurfacing of Town Hall Square during the 20th century.

Within the bedding layer for the surface of Town Hall Square was a fragment of a clay tobacco pipe, the design of which shows a crocodile in rushes wrapped around the bowl. The original pipe would also have included a reclining female figure with a dagger and hatchet on the stem. This particular pipe has been identified as one of the designs produced by the Manchester pipe maker Thomas Holland whose business flourished from the early 1870s until the early 1880s when he sold the company. Some interesting pottery was also recovered, with two fragments dated to *c.* 1813–34 featuring verses from the nursery rhyme Old Mother Hubbard. Other transfer-printed wares included 'field dots' type with oak leaf border dating from approximately 1820–50.

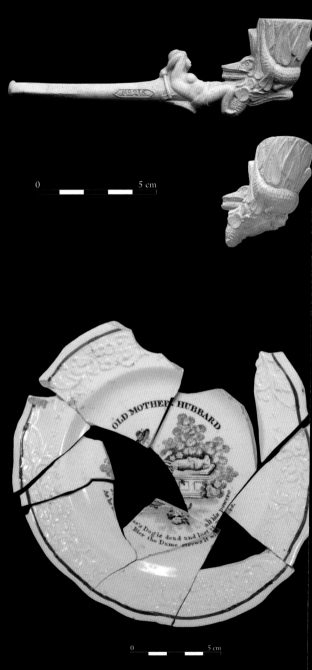

The second community excavation was carried out in July and August 2023 and was focused on four trenches placed across the Broadfield Park Slopes. The precise locations of these trenches were decided after a series of test pits had been opened to provide a glimpse of the depth and character of the archaeological remains. These test pits were excavated by a team of trainee archaeologists as part of a bespoke ten-week training programme delivered by GMAAS on behalf of the Rochdale Development Agency.

The three-week excavation, supported by the National Lottery Heritage Fund and supervised by GMAAS and the Slopes Dig Team, uncovered the substantial foundations of Charles Kershaw's 19th-century Central Corn Mill, which had been demolished in 1934. Earlier remains included historic surfaces associated with the former Leyland House that were discovered in a narrow trench placed slightly higher up the steep slope to the parish church. This trench lay adjacent to the ancient thoroughfare of the church steps and whilst medieval remains proved to be elusive, the excavation yielded fragments of 17th- and early 18th-century pottery and demonstrated a tantalising potential for earlier material to survive at a lower depth.

More than 1,000 people from local communities and schools engaged with each of the two excavations, either through direct participation or by taking advantage of the daily tours and open days that were offered. The majority of the participants had not taken part in an archaeological excavation previously and it was especially encouraging to see a large number of younger people becoming inspired by the quest to explore Rochdale's past. It is hoped that this groundswell of local appetite to engage with Rochdale's rich heritage and archaeology can gain momentum and continue to encourage the next generation of local archaeologists.

Opposite

Above: *Clay tobacco pipe with crocodile in rushes decoration, with a complete example for comparison (© University of Salford)*

Below: *White earthenware plate featuring verses from the nursey rhyme Old Mother Hubbard (© University of Salford)*

This page

A trench opened across the yard to Leyland House on the Broadfield Park Slopes in 2023 (© University of Salford)

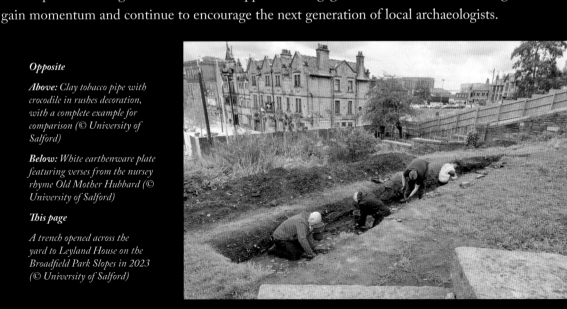

The late Victorian and Edwardian period was a time of optimism in Britain, in part due to another spell of expansion in the textile industry, although trade began to decline after the First World War. Nevertheless, Rochdale borough was classed as the third-largest centre for spinning in Britain until 1935, partially due to local manufacturers' adoption of innovative ring-spinning techniques and also because other areas had begun to suffer a greater decline in production. Successful companies, such as Kelsall & Kemp Ltd, which operated from Butts Mill on Smith Street, were able to expand their premises into neighbouring mill buildings such as Duncan Street Mill and Bowling Green Mill, both of which had become disused. The company's products were sold all over Britain as well as being exported under the 'Doctor' trademark. The firm shifted to manufacturing dress cloth with artificial fibres in the 1920s and became a leader in ladies' outer wear. Large new mills were also established on the periphery of Rochdale during this period, in places such as Spotland and Castleton.

In the town centre commercial ventures thrived and venues catering for new social activities, such as going to the cinema, sprung up, sometimes in obsolete civic buildings, like the old town hall, which became Andrew's Picture House in 1908. As well as mass entertainment, Rochdale's public transport infrastructure in the form of the now electrified tram network continued to develop with bridge coverings over the Roch forming a concourse at the junction of Smith Street, Drake Street and the Esplanade on which the tramway centre was

The tramway centre in foreground, with Butts Mill behind, c. 1905 (courtesy of Touchstones Rochdale)

The Park. Rochdale.

sited. After the First World War, a worldwide economic recession in 1920–21 struck Britain's export-dependent economy particularly hard, causing mass unemployment. However, as highlighted above, the textile industry in Rochdale did not go into decline until the 1930s when the Great Depression of 1929–41 caused numerous companies to go out of business.

Industrial and civic properties in Rochdale fell into disuse during the 1930s as a result of businesses closing, or because a lack of space in the congested town centre restricted the construction of larger buildings, causing expanding businesses to relocate elsewhere. For example, Duncan Street Mill was demolished, whilst the fire station on Alfred Street was closed and a new, larger station was constructed on McLure Road on the edge of the town centre. The public baths on Smith Street could not cater for increasing demand, so new baths were erected on Entwisle Road in 1937 to serve the rising population. The 1919 Housing Act required local councils to provide homes in areas of housing shortage, and early council estates were built on the outskirts of Rochdale in areas such as Kirkholt, Turf Hill, Clover Hall and Boarshaw. These developments represent the aspirations of the interwar housing boom, which sought to provide quality living spaces with large gardens, typified by the semi-detached house. The national policy on house building, with an increasing requirement for social housing, continued into the mid- to late 20th century and low-quality 19th-century terraced housing was replaced, for example at Lower Falinge.

Opposite top: 'The last steam tram to leave Rochdale, May 8, 1905'

Middle: A view of the G.L. Ashworth memorial in Broadfield Park from a postcard, c. 1914

Bottom: Drake Street, c. late 1930s

Other remnants of Rochdale's boom years had begun to disappear by the mid-20th century. The electric tram system was replaced by motor buses in the 1930s, the canal closed in 1952 and, due to a growing secularisation of society and a confluence of other factors including a reduction in the town centre's population, many chapels were closed with some repurposed for alternative uses. A Baptist chapel on Harriet Street had, by the mid-20th century, become a joinery works that ultimately saved the building from demolition.

The increasing number of redundant and obsolete buildings in the town centre presented opportunities for redevelopment, with many properties being demolished to make way for new civic structures such as the bus station, multi-storey car park, council offices and road-widening schemes, which radically altered the historic character of central Rochdale. This era of development, boosted by the opening of the A627(M) in 1972 and the resultant link to the M62 motorway, placed an emphasis on providing for private car usage and in so doing created a road gyratory system which left pedestrians feeling alienated as they were ushered onto aerial walkways. The Yorkshire Street regeneration necessitated the demolition of all of the shambles and market area ahead of the construction of the Rochdale Shopping Centre, which opened in 1978, and a retail park was established where the canal basin and surrounding industrial buildings had stood.

Left: The multi-storey car park from Smith Street c. 1970s (courtesy of Touchstones Rochdale)

Above: Red Lumb Mill in Norden in its current use for residential purposes

Below: Junction of Drake Street with South Parade, featuring the town hall and Broadfield Park Slopes to the rear, 1990s (© Paul Hogg)

The shift towards a retail and services-based economy signalled the start of the post-industrial era in the last third of the 20th century, causing mass unemployment and a rapid exodus of wealth from industrial centres. However, some textile production continued in Rochdale, for example at Alexander Drew Mill, Spotland where textile finishing took place, involving the bleaching, dyeing and printing of cloth. In some cases, former textile mills continued to be used for different industrial or commercial purposes, while some of the earlier mills have been converted for residential use, especially in more rural areas. However, a survey of extant mills in the Rochdale district commissioned by Historic England and carried out in 2017 by GMAAS found that there had been a high attrition rate of Rochdale's textile-mill heritage since the mid-1980s, when 229 standing mills were recorded in a similar survey; by 2017 only 102 still survived.

Over the last 20 years a new wave of redevelopment has swept through Rochdale, with the renewal and improvement or replacement of social housing on rundown estates while new houses have been constructed by private developers, often in partnership with the local authority. The old council offices and the multi-storey car park were demolished to build a new transport interchange that integrates a modern tram system with a bus interchange. The Rochdale Riverside development has sought to regenerate the town centre by delivering new retail, leisure and commercial premises, and by relieving the area of traffic. Much of Rochdale Town Hall Square had been given over to car parking and through traffic, but the square has recently resumed its intended function as a cherished area of public realm, reconnecting the town hall with the Grade 1-listed cenotaph and memorial gardens, Touchstones museum, and the historic bridge across the River Roch. This has been delivered in tandem with a Heritage Action Zone project that aimed to rejuvenate the distinctive built heritage on Drake Street to support the development of new communities and business opportunities. The net result of these major regeneration initiatives is a world-class setting for the town hall and a public space that will rival the best public squares in Europe.

The most recent round of redevelopment has roughly coincided with the introduction, in the early 1990s, of national guidelines presently covered by the National Planning Policy Framework, introduced in 2012. The inclusion of archaeologically related planning conditions within the planning process has, as this booklet demonstrates, led to an enormous increase in the amount of archaeological work that has taken place in Rochdale compared to before the 1990s. It has also meant that most of the archaeological investigations were funded by developers and undertaken by professional archaeologists. The various investigations that have taken place under the current planning regime were devised in consultation with GMAAS at the University of Salford. If any proposed new developments are likely to damage or remove buried archaeological remains, the curators at GMAAS can provide planning advice to Rochdale Borough Council on how to proceed.

When it is thought that archaeological remains may be impacted, developer-funded archaeological work is usually undertaken in several stages. Under normal circumstances, an archaeological consultant will carry out a desk-based assessment of the development site. Historic maps, photographs and documents, and the results of any historical or archaeological work in the vicinity of the development, are analysed to consider the potential for and likely survival of any archaeological remains. As part of this process, the Historic Environment Record – a digital record maintained by GMAAS that contains details of all known archaeological sites in Greater Manchester – will also be consulted.

If the desk-based assessment concludes that archaeological remains are likely to be present, an archaeological investigation will usually be recommended. Initially, this will entail an evaluation where a series of trial trenches will be excavated across the areas suggested by the desk-based assessment to have the potential to contain buried remains. The aim of this trenching is to determine the presence or absence of buried archaeological remains and, if present, to establish their character, date and state of preservation.

If the evaluation identifies any areas of the site with archaeologically significant remains which will be unavoidably affected by groundworks, then a further, more extensive phase of archaeological excavation may be recommended. During this phase of excavation, all the archaeological remains are recorded and all artefacts are collected. Following excavation, the records and artefacts are ordered, catalogued, analysed and interpreted. An illustrated excavation report and a site archive are then produced, which are eventually deposited with a local museum, and if the results are archaeologically significant, they will ultimately be published.

Professional archaeologists and volunteers take part in a community-led excavation at Rochdale Town Hall Square in 2021 (© University of Salford)

GLOSSARY

BRIGANTES: an Iron Age tribal political entity controlling much of what would become Northern England.

CARDING MACHINE: a machine used to disentangle, clean and intermix fibres to produce material suitable for subsequent processing.

DOMESDAY BOOK: a manuscript record of a survey of much of England and parts of Wales completed in 1086 by order of King William I. The king sent agents to survey every shire in England, to list his holdings and dues owed to him.

HENNEBIQUE SYSTEM: using steel bars to reinforce concrete slabs.

HUNTER-GATHERER: a catch-all term for a great diversity of subsistence practices finely tuned to local environmental conditions practised by communities who were likely nomadic. These groups procured food by foraging edible wild plants, insects, fungi, honey or anything safe to eat, and by hunting game. Hunter-gatherers contrast with more sedentary agricultural communities, which primarily depend on growing crops and keeping domesticated animals.

MADE GROUND: a layer of earth or rubble used to build up the ground level.

MOTTE AND BAILEY CASTLE: a rapidly built fortification consisting of two structures: a motte, which is a mound – often artificial – topped with a wooden or stone structure; and a bailey, a fortified enclosure situated next to the motte.

NIGHT SOIL: human excrement collected at night from buckets, cesspools and privies and sometimes used as manure.

NONCONFORMIST: a Protestant Christian who did not conform to the governance and usages of the established church, the Church of England (Anglican Church).

PACKHORSE TRAILS: routes used by packhorses to transport goods.

FURTHER READING

Fishwick, H, 1889 *History of the Parish of Rochdale in the County of Lancaster*, Rochdale

Gregory, R, 2019 'Yeoman Farmers and Handloom Weavers: The Archaeology of the Kingsway Business Park', *Greater Manchester's Past Revealed*, 23, Oxford Archaeology North, Lancaster

Gregory, R, Arrowsmith, P and Miller, I, 2021 *Farmers and Weavers: Investigation at Kingsway Business Park and Cutacre Country Park, Greater Manchester*, Oxford Archaeology North, Lancaster

Poole, SW, 2020 *The Use and Origin of Chert on Early Mesolithic sites in the Pennines and Rossendale*, unpublished

Wadsworth, AP, 1923–25 'History of the Rochdale Woollen trade' *Transactions of the Rochdale Literary and Science Society* 15, 90–110

Wild, AS, 1987 *Top O'Th' Steps: A History of St Chad's Parish Church, Rochdale*, St Chad's Educational Trust

Williams, M. with Fernie, DA, 1992 *Cotton Mills in Greater Manchester*, Preston

Copies of the detailed technical reports from the excavations referred to in this booklet have been deposited with the Greater Manchester Historic Environment Record.

Publications in the *Greater Manchester's Past Revealed* series are available from GMAAS within the University of Salford, and digital copies of all the volumes published between 2010 and 2021 can be downloaded by scanning the QR code below.

Acknowledgements

The production of this booklet has been funded entirely by Willmott Dixon Construction Limited as part of the Rochdale Riverside development.

Thanks are extended to Ian Miller, Lead Archaeologist at the Greater Manchester Archaeological Advisory Service (GMAAS), for providing valuable advice and access to unpublished excavation reports, and assistance with the production of this booklet. Also, to Lesley Dunkley of GMAAS for her assistance in providing unpublished reports and for proofreading the manuscript.

Many thanks are extended to Jenny Driver, Helen Beckett, Janet Byrne and everyone else who assisted with much patience at the Rochdale Arts and Heritage Resource Centre and the Local Studies Centre at Touchstones Rochdale. Especial thanks to Stephen Poole for his time spent explaining the long history of research on Rochdale's Mesolithic inhabitants and also for his invaluable knowledge of the Heritage Resource Centre's artefact collection. Thanks are also expressed to MOLA, and especially Kelly Griffiths and Blair Poole, for sharing their knowledge and images from the excavation of the Rochdale Canal Basin in 2022–23.

It would of course have been impossible to write this booklet and have an understanding of Rochdale's archaeology without the contributions made by the numerous archaeologists who worked on the various excavations and investigations over the years. Thanks are therefore due to those employees of Oxford Archaeology, the University of Manchester Archaeological Unit, Gifford, Royal Commission on the Historical Monuments of England, ArcHeritage, Archaeological Research Services, Nexus Heritage, L-P Archaeology and Salford Archaeology who contributed to investigations in Rochdale. Special mention is made of the Rochdale Development Agency team, particularly Emma Birkett, Emma Robinson and Natalie Oldham, for facilitating the community-led projects as part of the National Lottery Heritage Fund projects at Rochdale Town Hall and the Broadfield Park Slopes. The fieldwork was delivered by the Rochdale Slopes Dig Team of Lauren Davies, Helena Lambert, Alison Iveson, Penny Meadowcroft and Stephen Morley under the supervision of Dr Colin Elder from the University of Salford, and thanks are also due to everyone who has taken part in archaeological work in Rochdale.

Many of the historical images included in this booklet have been reproduced courtesy of Touchstones Rochdale, Rochdale Arts and Heritage Service. Oxford Archaeology provided images of the sites that they excavated, whilst MOLA and GMAAS have also kindly supplied some images of fieldwork projects they have carried out in Rochdale and the surrounding area.